Timeless Quotations on

HOPE

POCKET POSITIVES™

Timeless Quotations on

HOPE

Compiled by John Cook

Fairview Press
Minneapolis

Published by Fairview Press, 2450 Riverside Avenue South, Minneapolis, MN 55454.

Library of Congress Cataloging-in-Publication Data
Timeless quotations on hope / compiled by John Cook.
       p.   cm. -- (Pocket positives)
    ISBN 1-57749-059-2 (pbk.: alk. paper)
    1. Hope--Quotations, maxims, etc. I. Cook, John,
    1939–   . II. Series.
    BD216.T55   1997
    152.4--dc21   97-31318
                                                         CIP

First Printing: November 1997
Printed in the United States of America
01 00 99 98 97   7 6 5 4 3 2 1

Cover design: Laurie Duren

For a free catalogue, call toll-free 1–800–544–8207. Visit our web site at www.press.Fairview.org.

for Freddi, Blake, Brian, and Timmy

CONTENTS

INTRODUCTION

THE BOOKS IN THE POCKET POSITIVES™ SERIES originated as a selection of life-affirming quotations I compiled for my nephews and niece for Christmas 1989.

Because I was concerned that one of them was too young for it, I wrote in a letter that accompanied the collection, "just put it away in a safe place until you're ready for it." To address the question of how someone would know they were "ready," I wrote:

"You'll be ready the first time things don't go the way you want them to, the first time you doubt your ability to do something, the first time you're tempted to quit or give up, the first time you actually fail at something.

"You'll be ready the first time you doubt a friend, or think you can't trust anyone.

"You'll be ready the first time you have to make an important decision, or choice.

"You'll be ready the first time you're afraid of something, or worried.

"You'll know when you're ready. When you are, these thoughts should give you the courage and confidence and spirit you need ... and they'll remind you of the wonder and the joy of life, regardless of how dark things seem at the moment.

"I know they will.... They always have for me."

So, in addition to being a resource for researchers, writers, students, and professionals, I hope this book—and all the books in the Pocket Positives™ series—will provide comfort and inspiration for the casual browser or reader.

• • •

Numerous questions and concerns about accuracy confront anyone who compiles quotations. Take, for example, differences in the spelling of sources' names. The same famous Russian novelist has had his name spelled "Dostoevski," "Dostoievski," and "Dostoyevsky."

The formality required to identify sources is another issue. The Spanish Jesuit writer Baltasar Gracian Y Morales, for example, is more commonly referred to as "Baltasar Gracian," or simply "Gracian." And some sources are almost universally referred to by only one name, usually in the interest of brevity, and because it would be difficult to confuse them with anyone else. "Crebillion," for example, is used for Prosper Jolyot de Crebillion, the French dramatic poet.

And, of course, through the years many exact quotations—and even more that are very similar—have been attributed to more than one source.

I have made every effort to present each quotation as accurately as possible, and to recognize and honor the appropriate source. In particularly demanding situations, the language and sources cited are those most often used by other compilers and editors. Where it was impossible to verify the accuracy or source of a quotation, I have included it anyway if I believed that the usefulness of the quotation outweighed the demands of scholarly rigor.

PART ONE

HOPE

THE IMPORTANCE
AND VALUE OF HOPE

If it were not for hopes, the heart would break.

—Thomas Fuller

None are completely wretched but those who are without hope, and few are reduced so low as that.

—William Hazlitt

To all the living there is hope, for a living dog is better than a dead lion.

—Eccl. 9:4

Everybody lives for something better to come.

—Anon.

Hope is itself a species of happiness, and, perhaps, the chief happiness which this world affords.

—Samuel Johnson

At first we hope too much; later on, not enough.

—Joseph Roux

Lord save us all from ... a hope tree that has lost the faculty of putting out blossoms.

—Mark Twain

He who does not hope to win has already lost.

—José Joaquin Olmedo

We should not let our fears hold us back from pursuing our hopes.

—John F. Kennedy

Man needs, for his happiness, not only the enjoyment of this or that, but hope and enterprise and change.

—Bertrand Russell

Great hopes make great men.

—Thomas Fuller

In all pleasure hope is a considerable part.

—Samuel Johnson

It has never been, and never will be, easy work! But the road that is built in hope is more pleasant to the traveler than the road built in despair, even though they both lead to the same destination.

—Marian Zimmer Bradley

Without hope men are only half alive. With hope they dream and think and work.

—Charles Sawyer

A leader is a dealer in hope.

—Napoleon Bonaparte

They say a person needs just three things to be truly happy in this world. Someone to love, something to do, and something to hope for.

—Tom Bodett

Hope is one of those things in life you cannot do without.
—LeRoy Douglas

The important thing is not that we can live on hope alone, but that life is not worth living without it.
—Harvey Milk

Hope and patience are two sovereign remedies for all, the surest reposals, the softest cushions to lean on in adversity.
—Robert Burton

Optimism is the faith that leads to achievement. Nothing can be done without hope or confidence.
—Helen Keller

Our greatest good, and what we least can spare, is hope.
—John Armstrong

We want to create hope for the person ...
we must give hope, always hope.
—Mother Teresa, on AIDS

Take hope from the heart of man and
you make him a beast of prey.
—Ouida

Strong hope is a much greater stimulant
of life than any single realized joy could
be.
—Friedrich Nietzsche

And thou shalt be secure because there is
hope.
—Jb. 11:18

Hope! Of all the ills that men endure,
the only cheap and universal cure.
—Abraham Cowley

Hope is the last thing ever lost.
—Italian proverb

WITHOUT HOPE, WE DIE

Hope is the last thing that dies in man.
—Francois de La Rochefoucauld

Hope is the major weapon against the suicide impulse.
—Dr. Karl Menninger

Refusal to hope is nothing more than a decision to die.
—Bernie S. Siegel, M.D.

Man can live about forty days without food, about three days without water, about eight minutes without air ... but only for one second without hope.
—Hal Lindsey

To eat bread without hope is still slowly to starve to death.
—Pearl S. Buck

HOPE, FAITH, AND BELIEF

Now the God of hope fills you with all
joy and peace in believing, that ye may
abound in hope.

—Rom. 15:13

Hope is putting faith to work when
doubting would be easier.

—Anon.

Hope is the belief, more or less strong,
that joy will come; desire is the wish it
may come.

—Sydney Smith

There is nothing that fear or hope does
not make men believe.

—Vauvenargues

Hope is the parent of faith.

—C.A. Bartol

HOPE IS A GREAT MOTIVATOR

No hope, no action.
—Peter Levi

Hope is one of the principal springs that keep mankind in motion.
—Thomas Fuller

Hope arouses, as nothing else can arouse, a passion for the possible.
—William Sloan Coffin, Jr.

Hope is the anchor of the soul, the stimulus to action, and the incentive to achievement.
—Anon.

Hope is a vigorous principle ... it sets the head and heart to work, and animates a man to do his utmost.
—Jeremy Collier

HOPE AS A DREAM

Hope is the pillar that holds up the world. Hope is the dream of a waking man.

> —Pliny, the Elder

Hope is a waking dream.

> —Aristotle

Hope is but the dream of those that wake.

> —Matthew Prior

Hope is not a dream, but a way of making dreams become reality.

> —L.J. Cardina Suenens

In the night of death, hope sees a star, and listening love can hear the rustle of a wing.

> —Robert G. Ingersoll

HOPE AND HAPPINESS

Hope is grief's best music.

—Anon.

Hope is the last thing to abandon the unhappy.

—Anon.

The miserable have no medicine but hope.

—William Shakespeare

Hope is the second soul of the unhappy.

—Johann von Goethe

To hope is to enjoy.

—Jacques Delille

You have to believe in happiness, or happiness never comes.

—Douglas Malloch

HOPE AND THE FUTURE

Hope is the positive mode of awaiting
the future.

> —Emil Brunner

If we were logical, the future would be
bleak indeed. But we are more than
logical. We are human beings, and we
have faith, and we have hope, and we
can work.

> —Jacques Cousteau

If winter comes, can spring be far
behind?

> —Percy Bysshe Shelley

"Wait'll next year!" is the favorite cry of
baseball fans, football fans, hockey fans,
and gardeners.

> —Robert Orben

HOPE AND PATIENCE

Hope and patience are two sovereign
remedies for all, the surest reposals, the
softest cushions to lean on in adversity.
—Robert Burton

Patience is the art of hoping.
—Vauvenargues

Hope is patience with the lamp lit.
—Tertullian

All human wisdom is summed up in two
words—wait and hope.
—Alexandre Dumas

While there's life, there's hope.
—Terence

Hope sees the invisible, feels the intangi-
ble and achieves the impossible.
—Anon.

HOPE AND FEAR

Hope is some extraordinary spiritual
grace that God gives us to control our
fears, not to oust them.
—Vincent NcNabb

Where no hope is left, is left no fear.
—John Milton

There is no hope unmingled with fear,
and no fear unmingled with hope.
—Baruch Spinoza

I steer my bark with hope in my heart,
leaving fear astern.
—Thomas Jefferson

Hope is the power of being cheerful in
circumstances which we know to be desperate.
—G.K. Chesterton

HOPELESSNESS

When you say a situation or a person is
hopeless, you are slamming the door in
the face of God.
>   —Charles L. Allen

Hell is the place where one has ceased to
hope.
>   —A.J. Cronin

There are no hopeless situations; there
are only men who have grown hopeless
about them.
>   —Clare Boothe Luce

Hope never abandons you, you abandon
it.
>   —George Weinberg

Other men see only a hopeless end, but
the Christian rejoices in an endless hope.
>   —Gilbert M. Beeken

Primary Sources of Hope

Extreme hopes are born of extreme misery.

—Bertrand Russell

Hope is brightest when it dawns from fears.

—Sir Walter Scott

Hope is like a road in the country; there was never a road, but when many people walk on it, the road comes into existence.

—Lin Yutang

Hope works in these ways: it looks for the good in people instead of harping on the worst; it discovers what can be done instead of grumbling about what cannot; it regards problems, large or small, as opportunities; it pushes ahead when it would be easy to quit; it "lights the candle" instead of "cursing the darkness."

—Anon.

When you're depressed, the whole body is depressed, and it translates to the cellular level. The first objective is to get your energy up, and you can do it through play. It's one of the most powerful ways of breaking up hopelessness and bringing energy into the situation.

—O. Carl Simonton

Every area of trouble gives out a ray of hope, and the one unchangeable certainty is that nothing is certain or unchangeable.

—John F. Kennedy

Hope springs eternal in the human breast.

—Alexander Pope

Honor begets honor, trust begets trust, faith begets faith, and hope is the mainspring of life.

—Henry L. Stimson

OTHER DEFINITIONS OF HOPE

Hope is the poor man's bread.
—Gary Herbert

Oh, what a valiant faculty is hope.
—Michel de Montaigne

Hope is necessary in every condition.
The miseries of poverty, sickness and
captivity would, without this comfort, be
insupportable.
—Samuel Johnson

Hope is an adventure, a going forward, a
confident search for a rewarding life.
—Dr. Karl Menninger

Hope is the first thing to take some sort
of action.
—John Armstrong

Hope is a risk that must be run.
—Georges Bernanos

Appetite, with an opinion of attaining, is called hope; the same, without such opinion, despair.

—Thomas Hobbes

Hope is faith holding out its hand in the dark.

—George Iles

Hope is a satisfaction unto itself, and need not be fulfilled to be appreciated.

—Dr. Fred O. Henker

Hope is desire and expectation rolled into one.

—Ambrose Bierce

Hope, that star of life's tremulous ocean.

—Paul Moon James

Hope is the word which God has written on the brow of every man.

—Victor Hugo

Hope is the thing with feathers that perches in the soul and sings the tune without words and never stops at all.
　　　　　　　　　—Emily Dickinson

Hope is a very unruly emotion.
　　　　　　　　　—Gloria Steinem

True hope is swift and flies with swallow's wings;
Kings it makes Gods, and meaner creatures kings.
　　　　　　　　　—William Shakespeare

Hope is not the conviction that something will turn out well but the certainty that something makes sense, regardless of how it turns out.
　　　　　　　　　—Vaclav Havel

Hope is a light diet, but very stimulating.
　　　　　　　　　—Honore de Balzac

General Quotations about Hope

Hope, like the gleaming taper's light,
  adorns and cheers our way;
And still, as darker grows the night,
  emits a lighter ray.
                    —Oliver Goldsmith

Just as dumb creatures are snared by
food, human beings would not be caught
unless they had a nibble of hope.
                    —Petronius

Ten thousand men possess ten thousand
hopes.
                    —Euripides

Hope has as many lives as a cat or a king.
        —Henry Wadsworth Longfellow

In time of trouble avert not thy face from
hope, for the soft marrow abideth in the
hard bone.
                    —Hafez

Have hope. Though clouds environs
   now,
And gladness hides her face in scorn,
Put thou the shadow from thy brow—
No night but hath its morn.
              —J.C.F. von Schiller

There is no medicine like hope, no incentive so great, and no tonic so powerful as expectation of something tomorrow.
              —Orison Swett Marden

Faith, hope, and charity—if we had more of the first two, we'd need less of the last.
              —Anon.

In the face of uncertainty, there is nothing wrong with hope.
              —O. Carl Simonton

One should ... be able to see things as hopeless and yet be determined to make them otherwise.
              —F. Scott Fitzgerald

Hope is the only bee that makes honey
without flowers.

—Robert G. Ingersoll

They sailed. They sailed. Then spoke the
    mate:
"This mad sea shows its teeth to-night
He curls his lip, he lies in wait,
With lifted teeth, as if to bite!
Brave admiral, say but one good word:
What shall we do when hope is gone?"
The words leapt like a leaping sword:
    "Sail on! sail on! and on!"

—Joaquin Miller

The hopeful man sees success where others see failure, sunshine where others see
shadows and storm.

—Orison Swett Marden

The wind was cold off the mountains
and I was a naked man with enemies
behind me, and nothing before me but
hope.

—Louis L'Amour

I always entertain great hopes.

> —Robert Frost

To hope is not to demand.

> —Anon.

Hold your head high, stick your chest out. You can make it. It gets dark sometimes but morning comes.... Keep hope alive.

> —Jesse Jackson

Forgiving means to pardon the unpardonable,
Faith means believing the unbelievable,
And hoping means to hope when things are hopeless.

> —G.K. Chesterton

It is the around-the-corner brand of hope that prompts people to action, while the distant hope acts as an opiate.

> —Eric Hoffer

The gift we can offer others is so simple
a thing as hope.

—Daniel Berrigan

It's never too late—in fiction or in life—
to revise.

—Nancy Thayer

Never despair.

—Horace

Even the cry from the depths is an affir-
mation: why cry if there is no hint of
hope of hearing?

—Martin Marty

PART TWO

VISUALIZATION

VISION DOESN'T DEPEND
ON OUR EYES

Vision is the art of seeing things invisible.

—Jonathan Swift

You can't depend on your eyes when your imagination is out of focus.

—Mark Twain

Just because a man lacks the use of his eyes doesn't mean he lacks vision.

—Stevie Wonder

Who is the wise man? He who sees what's going to be born.

—Solomon

True vision is always twofold. It involves emotional comprehensions as well as physical perception.

—Ross Parmenter

WE DON'T ALL VISUALIZE
THE SAME THINGS

A genius is one who shoots at something
no one else can see—and hits it.

—Anon.

A fool sees not the same tree that a wise
man sees.

—William Blake

A feeble man can see the farms that are
fenced and tilled, the houses that are
built. The strong man sees the possible
houses and farms. His eye makes estates
as fast as the sun breeds clouds.

—Ralph Waldo Emerson

Guido the plumber and Michelangelo
obtained their marble from the same
quarry, but what each saw in the marble
made the difference between a noble-
man's sink and a brilliant sculpture.

—Bob Kall

WE MUST VISUALIZE BEFORE
WE ACT OR CREATE

All acts performed in the world begin in
the imagination.

—Barbara Grizzuti Harrison

A rock pile ceases to be a rock pile the
moment a single man contemplates it,
bearing within him the image of a cathe-
dral.

—Antoine de Saint-Exupery

Man can only become what he is able to
consciously imagine, or to "image forth."

—Dane Rudhyar

Before you begin a thing remind yourself
that difficulties and delays quite impossible to foresee are ahead.... You can only
see one thing clearly, and that is your
goal. Form a mental vision of that and
cling to it through thick and thin.

—Kathleen Norris

VISUALIZATION AND DREAMS

Nothing happens unless first a dream.
> —Carl Sandburg

Where much is expected from an individual, he may rise to the level of events and make the dream come true.
> —Elbert Hubbard

The moment of enlightenment is when a person's dreams of possibilities become images of probabilities.
> —Vic Braden

Reach high, for stars lie hidden in your soul. Dream deep, for every dream precedes the goal.
> —Pamela Vaull Starr

Dream lofty dreams, and as you dream, so shall you become. Your vision is the promise of what you shall at last unveil.
> —John Ruskin

When we can't dream any longer, we die.
—Emma Goldman

Hold fast to dreams, for if dreams die,
life is a broken-winged bird that cannot
fly.
—Langston Hughes

Dream lofty dreams, and as you dream,
so shall you become. Your vision is the
promise of what you shall at last unveil.
—John Ruskin

It may be that those who do most, dream
most.
—Stephen Leacock

If one advances confidently in the direction of his dreams, and endeavors to live
the life which he has imagined, he will
meet with a success unexpected in common hours.
—Henry David Thoreau

General Quotations about Vision

Imagination has always had powers of resurrection that no science can match.
— Ingrid Bengis

A person can grow only as much as his horizon allows.
— John Powell

When there is no vision, people perish.
— Ralph Waldo Emerson

Man can only receive what he sees himself receiving.
— Florence Scovel Shinn

A couple of times a day I sit quietly and visualize my body fighting the AIDS virus. It's the same as me sitting and seeing myself hit the perfect serve. I did that often when I was an athlete.
— Arthur Ashe

Is life so wretched? Isn't it rather your hands which are too small, your vision which is muddled? You are the one who must grow up.

—Dag Hammarskjold

The artist doesn't see things as they are, but as he is.

—Anon.

We all live under the same sky, but we don't all have the same horizon.

—Konrad Adenauer

Five minutes, just before going to sleep, given to a bit of directed imagination regarding achievement possibilities of the morrow, will steadily and increasingly bear fruit, particularly if all ideas of difficulty, worry or fear are resolutely ruled out and replaced by those of accomplishment and smiling courage.

—Frederick Pierce

You can vitally influence your life from within by auto-suggestion. The first thing each morning, and the last thing each night, suggest to yourself specific ideas that you wish to embody in your character and personality. Address such suggestions to yourself, silently or aloud, until they are deeply impressed upon your mind.

—Grenville Kleiser

Leaders are visionaries with a poorly developed sense of fear and no concept of the odds against them. They make the impossible happen.

—Dr. Robert Jarvik

PART THREE

POSITIVE THINKING

OUR ATTITUDES CREATE OUR LIVES

Man is what he believes.
>—Anton Chekhov

Believe that life is worth living, and your belief will help create that fact.
>—William James

When you look at the world in a narrow way, how narrow it seems! When you look at it in a mean way, how mean it is! When you look at it selfishly, how selfish it is! But when you look at it in a broad, generous, friendly spirit, what wonderful people you find in it.
>—Horace Rutledge

What one believes to be true either is true or becomes true within limits to be found experientially and experimentally. These limits are beliefs to be transcended.
>—John Lilly

Our belief at the beginning of a doubtful undertaking is the one thing that ensures the successful outcome of our venture.

—William James

If you constantly think of illness, you eventually become ill; if you believe yourself to be beautiful, you become so.

—Shakti Gawain

The greatest discovery of my generation is that man can alter his life simply by altering his attitude of mind.

—William James

Immense power is acquired by assuring yourself in your secret reveries that you were born to control affairs.

—Andrew Carnegie

If you keep on saying things are going to be bad, you have a good chance of being a prophet.

—Isaac Bashevis Singer

The thing always happens that you really believe in; and the belief in a thing makes it happen.

—Frank Lloyd Wright

We are what we believe we are.

—Benjamin N. Cardozo

Each of us makes his own weather, determines the color of the skies in the emotional universe which he inhabits.

—Fulton J. Sheen

Man's rise or fall, success or failure, happiness or unhappiness depends on his attitude ... a man's attitude will create the situation he imagines.

—James Lane Allen

Man's real life is happy, chiefly because he is ever expecting that it soon will be so.

—Edgar Allan Poe

'Tis very certain the desire of life pro-
longs it.

—Lord Byron

Could we change our attitude, we
should not only see life differently, but
life itself would come to be different.
Life would undergo a change of appear-
ance because we ourselves had under-
gone a change in attitude.

—Katherine Mansfield

If you expect nothing, you're apt to be
surprised. You'll get it.

—Malcolm Forbes

The words "I am ..." are potent words;
be careful what you hitch them to. The
thing you're claiming has a way of reaching back and claiming you.

—A.L. Kitselman

They can because they think they can.

—Virgil

Self-image sets the boundaries of individual accomplishment.

—Maxwell Maltz

Nothing can stop the man with the right mental attitude from achieving his goal; nothing on earth can help the man with the wrong mental attitude.

—W.W. Ziege

Since the human body tends to move in the direction of its expectations—plus or minus—it is important to know that attitudes of confidence and determination are no less a part of the treatment program than medical science and technology.

—Norman Cousins

To the timid and hesitating everything is impossible because it seems so.

—Sir Walter Scott

WE FIND WHAT WE LOOK FOR

What we see depends mainly on what we look for.

—John Lubbock

People only see what they are prepared to see.

—Ralph Waldo Emerson

Look for the ridiculous in everything and you find it.

—Jules Renard

The more wary you are of danger, the more likely you are to meet it.

—Jean de La Fontaine

He that seeks trouble always finds it.

—English proverb

We are always paid for our suspicion by finding what we suspect.

—Henry David Thoreau

The unthankful heart ... discovers no mercies; but the thankful heart ... will find, in every hour, some heavenly blessings.

—Henry Ward Beecher

If you are possessed by an idea, you find it expressed everywhere, you even smell it.

—Thomas Mann

All seems infected that the infected spy, as all looks yellow to the jaundiced eye.

—Alexander Pope

The faultfinder will find faults even in paradise.

—Henry David Thoreau

Those see nothing but faults that seek for nothing else.

—Thomas Fuller

LIFE IS LIKE A MIRROR

Life is a mirror and will reflect back to
the thinker what he thinks into it.
—Ernest Holmes

The world is a looking glass and gives
back to every man the reflection of his
own face. Frown at it and it will in turn
look sourly upon you; laugh at it and
with it, and it is a jolly, kind companion.
—William Makepeace Thackeray

The world is a great mirror. If you are
loving, if you are friendly, if you are
helpful, the world will prove loving and
friendly and helpful to you. The world
is what you are.
—Thomas Dreier

The world is like a mirror; frown at it,
and it frowns at you. Smile and it
smiles, too.
—Herbert Samuels

OUR THOUGHTS DETERMINE OUR LIVES

Our minds can shape the way a thing
will be because we act according to our
expectations.

—Federico Fellini

The way a man's mind runs is the way he
is sure to go.

—Henry B. Wilson

The happiness of your life depends upon
the quality of your thoughts ... take care
that you entertain no notions unsuitable
to virtue and reasonable nature.

—Marcus Aurelius

All that a man does outwardly is but the
expression and completion of his inward
thought. To work effectively, he must
think clearly; to act nobly, he must
think nobly.

—William Ellery Channing

You cannot escape the results of your thoughts.... Whatever your present environment may be, you will fall, remain or rise with your thoughts, your vision, your ideal. You will become as small as your controlling desire, as great as your dominant aspiration.

—James Lane Allen

The life each of us lives is the life within the limits of our own thinking. To have life more abundant, we must think in limitless terms of abundance.

—Thomas Dreier

A man is literally what he thinks.

—James Lane Allen

Nothing befalls us that is not of the nature of ourselves. There comes no adventure but wears to our soul the shape of our everyday thoughts.

—Maurice Maeterlinck

All that we are is the result of what we have thought. The mind is everything. What we think, we become.

—Buddha

I believe that if you think about disaster, you will get it. Brood about death and you hasten your demise. Think positively and masterfully with confidence and faith, and life becomes more secure, more fraught with action, richer in achievement and experience.

—Eddie Rickenbacker

Think you can, think you can't; either way, you'll be right.

—Henry Ford

Our destiny changes with our thoughts; we shall become what we wish to become, do what we wish to do, when our habitual thoughts correspond with our desires.

—Orison Swett Marden

Before a painter puts a brush to his canvas he sees his picture mentally.... If you think of yourself in terms of a painting, what do you see?... Is the picture one you think worth painting?... You create yourself in the image you hold in your mind.

—Thomas Dreier

Our best friends and our worst enemies are our thoughts. A thought can do us more good than a doctor or a banker or a faithful friend. It can also do us more harm than a brick.

—Dr. Frank Crane

A man's life is what his thoughts make it.

—Marcus Aurelius

A man is what he thinks about all day long.

—Ralph Waldo Emerson

If you think it's going to rain, it will.

—Clint Eastwood

The mere apprehension of a coming evil
has put many into a situation of the
utmost danger.

—Lucan

The soul contains the event that shall
befall it, for the event is only the actual-
ization of its thoughts, and what we pray
to ourselves for is always granted.

—Ralph Waldo Emerson

As you think, you travel, and as you love,
you attract. You are today where your
thoughts have brought you; you will be
tomorrow where your thoughts take you.

—James Lane Allen

God will help you if you try, and you can
if you think you can.

—Anna Delaney Peale

To expect defeat is nine-tenths of defeat
itself.

—Francis Marion Crawford

The quality of our expectations determines the quality of our action.
—André Godin

What a man thinks of himself, that is what determines, or rather indicates, his fate.
—Henry David Thoreau

Man, being made reasonable, and so a thinking creature, there is nothing more worthy of his being than the right direction and employment of his thoughts; since upon this depends both his usefulness to the public, and his own present and future benefit in all respects.
—William Penn

Never think any oldish thoughts. It's oldish thoughts that make a person old.
—James A. Farley

They can because they think they can.
—Virgil

As a man thinketh, so is he, and as a
man chooseth, so is he.

—Bible

Thoughts lead on to purposes; purposes
go forth in action; actions form habits;
habits decide character; and character
fixes our destiny.

—Tyron Edwards

Keep your thoughts right, for as you
think, so are you. Therefore, think only
those things that will make the world
better, and you unashamed.

—Henry H. Buckley

Great men are they who see that the spiritual is stronger than any material force,
that thoughts rule the world.

—Ralph Waldo Emerson

Baseball is 90 percent mental. The other
half is physical.

—Yogi Berra

Every man is free to rise as far as he's able or willing, but the degree to which he thinks determines the degree to which he'll rise.

—Ayn Rand

What you think means more than anything else in your life.

—George Matthew Adams

There comes no adventure but wears to our soul the shape of our everyday thoughts.

—Maurice Maeterlinck

Change your thoughts and you change your world.

—Norman Vincent Peale

The way in which we think of ourselves has everything to do with how our world sees us.

—Arlene Raven

Be careful of your thoughts; they may become words at any moment.
—Ira Gassen

The wisdom of all ages and cultures emphasizes the tremendous power our thoughts have over our character and circumstances.
—Liane Cordes

Events, circumstances, etc. have their origin in ourselves. They spring from seeds which we have sown.
—Henry David Thoreau

If we live good lives, the times are also good. As we are, such are the times.
—Saint Augustine

Man does not simply exist, but always decides what his existence will be, what he will become in the next moment.
—Viktor Frankel

OUR THOUGHTS DETERMINE OUR HAPPINESS

We exaggerate misfortune and happiness alike. We are never either so wretched or so happy as we say we are.

—Honore de Balzac

We are never so happy or so unhappy as we think.

—Francois de La Rochefoucauld

The greater part of our happiness or misery depends on our dispositions, and not our circumstances.

—Martha Washington

Man is only miserable so far as he thinks himself so.

—Sannazare

A man's as miserable as he thinks he is.

—Marcus Annaeus Seneca

The most unhappy of all men is he who
believes himself to be so.

—David Hume

The mind is its own place, and in itself
can make a heaven of hell, a hell of
heaven.

—John Milton

All happiness is in the mind.

—Anon.

Happiness is not a matter of events, it
depends upon the tides of the mind.

—Alice Meynell

I am happy and content because I think I
am.

—Alain-Rene Lesage

A happy life consists in tranquility of
mind.

—Cicero

The happiest person is the person who
thinks the most interesting thoughts.
                    —William Lyon Phelps

Unhappiness indicates wrong thinking,
just as ill health indicates a bad regimen.
                    —Paul Bourge

The pessimist sees the difficulty in every
opportunity; the optimist sees the opportunity in every difficulty.
                    —L.P. Jacks

Happiness does not depend on outward
things, but on the way we see them.
                    —Leo Tolstoy

Happiness will never be any greater than
the idea we have of it.
                    —Maurice Maeterlinck

He is happy that knoweth not himself to
be otherwise.
                    —Thomas Fuller

Misery is almost always the result of thinking.

—Joseph Joubert

Like begets like; honesty begets honesty; trust, trust; and so on.

—James F. Bell

A great obstacle to happiness is to expect too much happiness.

—Bernard de Fontenelle

The pessimist is half-licked before he starts.

—Thomas A. Buckner

It isn't our position, but our disposition, that makes us happy.

—Anon.

We create our fate every day ... most of the ills we suffer from are directly traceable to our own behavior.

—Henry Miller

OUR THOUGHTS AFFECT OUR
BODIES AND OUR HEALTH

Some patients I see are actually draining
into their bodies the diseased thoughts of
their minds.

—Zachary T. Bercovitz, M.D.

The body manifests what the mind har-
bors.

—Jerry Augustine

You can promote your healing by your
thinking.

—James E. Sweeney

Since the human body tends to move in
the direction of its expectations—plus
or minus—it is important to know that
attitudes of confidence and determination are no less a part of the treatment
program than medical science and technology.

—Norman Cousins

We can destroy ourselves by cynicism
and disillusion, just as affectively as by
bombs.

—Kenneth Clark

When people asked, I used to tell them
how sick I was. The more I talked about
being sick, the worse I got. Finally, I
started saying, "I'm getting better." It
took a while, but then I started to feel
better, too.

—Michael Hirsch, person with AIDS

Most of the time we think we're sick it's
all in the mind.

—Thomas Wolfe

If you prepare for old age, old age comes
sooner.

—Anon.

I am dying, but otherwise I am quite
well.

—Edith Sitwell,
when asked how she felt

NEGATIVE, CYNICAL, PESSIMISTIC THINKING IS DANGEROUS

No one can defeat us unless we first defeat ourselves.
—Dwight D. Eisenhower

There are people who have an appetite for grief; pleasure is not strong enough and they crave pain. They have mithridatic stomachs which must be fed on poisoned bread, natures so doomed that no prosperity can sooth their ragged and dishevelled desolation.
—Ralph Waldo Emerson

You can't pay attention to your mistakes. I made a mistake today, I made a mistake yesterday. I think it's ... very important to ignore the negative.
—Jerry Rubin

I don't believe in pessimism.
—Clint Eastwood

You can't be pessimistic, because there are
so many things that go wrong every day
that if you were to be negative or pessimistic, you'd go out of business.
—John DePasquale

One of the most devastating experiences
in human life is disillusionment.
—Art Sisson

No pessimist ever discovered the secrets
of the stars, or sailed to an uncharted
land, or opened a new heaven to the
human spirit.
—Helen Keller

Cynicism is intellectual dandyism.
—George Meredith

When one door of happiness closes,
another opens; but often we look so long
at the closed door that we do not see the
one which has been opened for us.
—Helen Keller

WE ARE RESPONSIBLE
FOR OUR THOUGHTS

If we are not responsible for the
thoughts that pass our doors, we are at
least responsible for those we admit and
entertain.
> —Charles B. Newcomb

Optimism is an intellectual choice.
> —Diana Schneider

Think of only three things: your God,
your family and the Green Bay Packers—
in that order.
> —Vince Lombardi, to his team

We must dare to think unthinkable
thoughts.
> —James W. Fulbright

Politeness is the art of choosing among
one's real thoughts.
> —Abel Stevens

Your imagination has much to do with
your life.... It is for you to decide how
you want your imagination to serve you.
—Philip Conley

A vacant mind invites dangerous
inmates, as a deserted mansion tempts
wandering outcasts to enter and take up
their abode in its desolate apartments.
—Hilliard

Great things are not something acciden-
tal, but must certainly be willed.
—Vincent van Gogh

A person who doubts himself is like a
man who would enlist in the ranks of
his enemies and bear arms against himself. He makes his failure certain by
himself being the first person to be convinced of it.

—Alexandre Dumas

THE IMPORTANCE AND VALUE OF POSITIVE THINKING

Optimism is essential to achievement and is also the foundation of courage and of true progress.

—Nicholas Murray Butler

If I were to wish for anything, I should not wish for wealth and power, but for the passionate sense of the potential, for the eye which, ever young and ardent, sees the possible ... what wine is so sparkling, so fragrant, so intoxicating, as possibility!

—Søren Kierkegaard

What after all has maintained the human race on this old globe, despite all the calamities of nature and all the tragic failings of mankind, if not the faith in new possibilities and the courage to advocate them?

—Jane Adams

The basic success orientation is having an optimistic attitude.

—John DePasquale

The biggest quality in successful people, I think, is an impatience with negative thinking ... my feeling was, even if it's as bad as I think it is, we'll make it work.

—Edward McCabe

It doesn't hurt to be optimistic. You can always cry later.

—Lucimar Santos de Lima

Positive thinking is the key to success in business, education, pro football, anything that you can mention. I go out there thinking that I am going to complete every pass.

—Ron Jaworski

There is in the worst of fortune the best of chances for a happy change.

—Euripides

Optimism and humor are the grease and glue of life. Without both of them we would never have survived our captivity.
—Philip Butler, Vietnam POW

Optimism is the faith that leads to achievement. Nothing can be done without hope and confidence.
—Helen Keller

Think positively and masterfully, with confidence and faith, and life becomes more secure, more fraught with action, richer in achievement and experience.
—Eddie Rickenbacker

I cannot discover that anyone knows enough to say definitely what is and what is not possible.
—Henry Ford

I have learned to use the word impossible with the greatest caution.
—Wernher von Braun

The Wright brothers flew right through the smoke screen of impossibility.
>—Charles Franklin Kettering

On the human chessboard, all moves are possible.
>—Miriam Schiff

Every noble work is at first impossible.
>—Thomas Carlyle

In the long run, the pessimist may be proved to be right, but the optimist has a better time on the trip.
>—Daniel L. Reardon

I believe that ... all that can be, will be, if man helps.
>—André Gide

Optimism, unaccompanied by personal effort, is merely a state of mind and not fruitful.
>—Edward L. Curtis

WE CREATE OUR OWN SITUATIONS
AND CIRCUMSTANCES

Honor begets honor; trust begets trust;
faith begets faith; and hope is the mainspring of life.
>   —Henry L. Stimson

Hope is like a road in the country; there
was never a road, but when many people
walk on it, the road comes into existence.
>   —Lin Yutang

If fear is cultivated it will become
stronger, if faith is cultivated it will
achieve mastery.
>   —John Paul Jones

A human being fashions his consequences as surely as he fashions his goods
or his dwelling. Nothing that he says,
thinks or does is without consequences.
>   —Norman Cousins

All things are possible until they are proved impossible—and even the impossible may only be so as of now.

—Pearl S. Buck

Thousands upon thousands are yearly brought into a state of real poverty by their great anxiety not to be thought poor.

—William Cobbett

It seems to me probably that any one who has a series of intolerable positions to put up with must have been responsible for them to some extent ... they have contributed to it by impatience or intolerance, or brusqueness—or some provocation.

—Robert Hugh Benson

Opportunities multiply as they are seized; they die when neglected. Life is a long line of opportunities.

—John Wicker

I have found that if you love life, life will love you back.

—Arthur Rubinstein

The world has a way of giving what is demanded of it. If you are frightened and look for failure and poverty, you will get them, no matter how hard you may try to succeed. Lack of faith in yourself, in what life will do for you, cuts you off from the good things of the world. Expect victory and you make victory. Nowhere is this truer than in business that is, where bravery and faith bring both material and spiritual rewards.

—Preston Bradley

We are made kind by being kind.

—Eric Hoffer

Kindness gives birth to kindness.

—Sophocles

In Many Cases, We Determine What Will Happen to Us

We choose our joys and sorrows long
before we experience them.
—Kahlil Gibran

A man is a method, a progressive
arrangement; a selecting principle, gathering his like unto him wherever he goes.
What you are comes to you.
—Ralph Waldo Emerson

The principle of life is that life responds
by corresponding; your life becomes the
thing you have decided it shall be.
—Raymond Charles Barker

If we choose to be no more than clods of
clay, then we shall be used as clods of
clay for braver feet to tread on.
—Marie Corelli

WHAT WE PREPARE FOR
OFTEN HAPPENS

Preparing for the worst is an activity I
have taken up since I turned thirty-five,
and the worst actually began to happen.
>—Delia Ephron

What we prepare for is what we shall get.
>—William Graham Sumner

If you expect nothing, you're apt to be
surprised. You'll get it.
>—Malcolm Forbes

Debt is a trap which man sets and baits
himself, and then deliberately gets into.
>—Josh Billings

If one asks for success and prepares for
failure, he will get the situation he has
prepared for.
>—Florence Scovel Shinn

Whoso diggeth a pit shall fall therein.
—Prv. 26:27

The world has a way of giving what is
demanded of it. If you are frightened and
look for failure and poverty, you will get
them, no matter how hard you may try
to succeed. Lack of faith in yourself, in
what life will do for you, cuts you off
from the good things of the world.
Expect victory and you make victory.
Nowhere is this truer than in business
life, where bravery and faith bring both
material and spiritual rewards.
—Preston Bradley

Self-image sets the boundaries of individual accomplishment.
—Maxwell Maltz

Persistent prophecy is a familiar way of
assuring the event.
—George R. Gissing

The words "I am ..." are potent words;
be careful what you hitch them to. The
thing you're claiming has a way of reaching back and claiming you.

—A.L. Kitselman

If you keep saying things are going to be
bad, you have a good chance of being a
prophet.

—Isaac Bashevis Singer

We are what we pretend to be, so we
must be careful about what we pretend
to be.

—Kurt Vonnegut

Those who foresee the future and recognize it as tragic are often seized by a
madness which forces them to commit
the very acts which makes it certain that
what they dread shall happen.

—Dame Rebecca West

WE GET OUT OF LIFE WHAT WE PUT INTO IT

Men will get no more out of life than they put into it.

—William J.H. Boetcker

Whatsoever a man soweth, that shall he also reap.

—Gal. 6:7

There is a very real relationship, both quantitatively and qualitatively, between what you contribute and what you get out of this world.

—Oscar Hammerstein II

If a man plants melons he will reap melons; if he sows beans, he will reap beans.

—Chinese proverb

He who sows courtesy reaps friendship, and he who plants kindness gathers love.

—Saint Basil

WE DETERMINE HOW OTHER
PEOPLE RELATE TO US

Trust men and they will be true to you;
treat them greatly and they will show
themselves great.
—Ralph Waldo Emerson

We awaken in others the same attitude of
mind we hold toward them.
—Elbert Hubbard

Any man will usually get from other men
just what he is expecting of them. If he is
looking for friendship he will likely
receive it. If his attitude is that of indifference, it will beget indifference. And if
a man is looking for a fight, he will in all
likelihood be accommodated in that.
—John Richelsen

He who has not faith in others shall find
no faith in them.
—Lao-tzu

Give to the world the best you have and
the best will come back to you.
—Madeline Bridges

To make the world a friendly place, one
must show it a friendly face.
—James Whitcomb Riley

If you would be loved, love and be lov-
able.
—Benjamin Franklin

People are not going to love you unless
you love them.
—Pat Carroll

Getting people to like you is merely the
other side of liking them.
—Norman Vincent Peale

People, by and large, will relate to the
image you project.
—Chyatee

SELF-DOUBT WILL CREATE
THE VERY FAILURE WE FEAR

He who fears he shall suffer, already suffers what he fears.
> —Michel de Montaigne

Fear to let fall a drop and you spill a lot.
> —Malay proverb

To be ambitious for wealth, and yet always expecting to be poor; to be always doubting your ability to get what you long for, is like trying to reach east by travelling west. There is no philosophy which will help a man to succeed when he is always doubting his ability to do so, and thus attracting failure. No matter how hard you work for success, if your thought is saturated with the fear of failure, it will kill your efforts, neutralize your endeavors and make success impossible.
> —Charles Baudouin

The thing we fear we bring to pass.
　　　　　　　　—Elbert Hubbard

He who fears being conquered is sure of defeat.
　　　　　　　　—Napoleon Bonaparte

Dangers by being despised grow great.
　　　　　　　　—Edmund Burke

Doubt breeds doubt.
　　　　　　　　—Franz Grillparzer

Proust has pointed out that the predisposition to love creates its own objects; is this not also true of fear?
　　　　　　　　—Elizabeth Bowen

There are certain people who so ardently and passionately desire a thing, that from dread of losing it they leave nothing undone to make them lose it.
　　　　　　　　—Jean de La Bruyere

PEOPLE OFTEN BECOME WHAT IS EXPECTED OF THEM

A great manager has a knack for making ballplayers think they are better than they think they are. He forces you to have a good opinion of yourself. He lets you know he believes in you. He makes you get more out of yourself. And once you learn how good you really are, you never settle for playing anything less than your very best.

—Reggie Jackson

If you want your children to improve, let them overhear the nice things you say about them to others.

—Haim Ginott

Treat people as if they were what they should be, and you help them become what they are capable of becoming.

—Johann von Goethe

The only way to make a man trustworthy is to trust him.

—Henry L. Stimson

Children are likely to live up to what you believe of them.

—Lady Bird Johnson

However much we guard against it, we tend to shape ourselves in the image others have of us.

—Eric Hoffer

It is the nature of man to rise to greatness if greatness is expected of him.

—John Steinbeck

I dare you to be the strongest boy in this class.

—William H. Danforth's teacher

Men have a trick of coming up to what is expected of them, good or bad.

—Jacob Riis

Act "As If"

If you act like you're rich, you'll get rich.
— Adnan Koashoggi

To keep our faces toward change, and behave like free spirits in the presence of fate, is strength undefeatable.
— Helen Keller

We planted flowers last year, and I didn't know if I'd be alive to see them come up.
— Neal McHugh, person with AIDS

Act as if it were impossible to fail.
— Dorothea Brande

If you want a quality, act as if you already had it.
— William James

If you would be powerful, pretend to be powerful.
— Horne Tooke

Assume a virtue, if you have it not.
>—William Shakespeare

Act so as to elicit the best in others and thereby in thyself.
>—Felix Adler

We must laugh before we are happy, for fear of dying without having laughed at all.
>—Jean de La Bruyere

If you want to be a big company tomorrow, you have to start acting like one today.
>—Thomas Watson

Act as if you were already happy, and that will tend to make you happy.
>—Dale Carnegie

Always imitate the behavior of the winner when you lose.
>—Anon.

I couldn't hit a wall with a sixgun, but I can twirl one. It looks good.

—John Wayne

It is good to act as if. It is even better to grow to the point where it is no longer an act.

—Charles Caleb Colton

Practice being excited.

—Bill Foster

It is easy enough to be pleasant, when life flows by like a song. But the man worthwhile is one who will smile, when everything goes dead wrong.

—Ella Wheeler Wilcox

Attempt easy tasks as if they were difficult, and difficult as if they were easy; in the one case that confidence may not fall asleep, in the other that it may not be dismayed.

—Baltasar Gracian

It is best to act with confidence, no matter how little right you have to it.

> —Lillian Hellman

To find oneself jilted is a blow to one's pride. One must do one's best to forget it and if one doesn't succeed, at least one must pretend to.

> —Moliere

If you've got it, flaunt it. If you do not, pretend.

> —Wally Phillips

If you wish to live a life free from sorrow, think of what is going to happen as if it had already happened.

> —Epictetus

If I had a party to attend and didn't want to be there, I would play the part of someone who was having a lovely time.

> —Shirley MacLaine

To establish oneself in the world, one has to do all one can to appear established.

—Francois de La Rochefoucauld

To believe in God is to yearn for His existence, and furthermore, it is to act as if He did exist.

—Miguel de Unamuno

Our deeds determine us, as much as we determine our deeds.

—George Eliot

Illusory joy is often worth more than genuine sorrow.

—Rene Descartes

Live as if you like yourself, and it may happen.

—Marge Piercy

Make your judgement trustworthy by trusting it.

—Grenville Kleiser

Fake feeling good…. You're going to have to learn to fake cheerfulness. Believe it or not, eventually that effort will pay off: you'll actually start feeling happier.

—Jean Bach

I long to accomplish a great and noble task, but it is my chief duty to accomplish small tasks as if they were great and noble.

—Helen Keller

As is our confidence, so is our capacity.

—William Hazlitt

We become just by performing just actions, temperate by performing temperate actions, brave by performing brave actions.

—Aristotle

Think like a man of action, act like a man of thought.

—Henri Bergson

SOME INCREDIBLY
POSITIVE APPROACHES

They've got us surrounded again, the
poor bastards.
        —General Creighton W. Abrams

I'll just hit the dry side of the ball.
                —Stan Musial,
            on how to handle a spitball

My disease is one of the best things that
has happened to me; it has pulled me out
of a quietly desperate life toward one full
of love and hope.
    —Tom O'Connor, person with ARC

Retreat? We're coming out of here as a
Marine division. We're bringing our
equipment ... our wounded ... our dead.
Retreat, hell! We're just advancing in
another direction.
            —General Oliver Prince Smith

I'm in a wonderful position: I'm
unknown, I'm underrated, and there's
nowhere to go but up.
>
> —Pierre S. DuPont IV

My center is giving way, my right is in
retreat: situation excellent. I am attacking.
>
> —Marshal Ferdinand Foch

Focus is important. Focus on those parts
of yourself that are working. Look at
yourself as someone whose body is in the
process of healing. Concentrate on the
positive parts.
>
> —Will Garcia, person with AIDS

We are so outnumbered there's only one
thing to do. We must attack.
>
> —Sir Andrew Cunningham

Anyone can have an off decade.
>
> —Larry Cole

I've never been poor, only broke. Being poor is a frame of mind. Being broke is a temporary situation.

—Mike Todd

I can't say I was ever lost, but I was bewildered once for three days.

—Daniel Boone

Sunshine is delicious, rain is refreshing, wind braces us up, snow is exhilarating; there is really no such thing as bad weather, only different kinds of good weather.

—John Ruskin

If they do kill me, I shall never die another death.

—Abraham Lincoln

Circumstances—what are circumstances? I make circumstances.

—Napoleon Bonaparte

Disease can be seen as a call for personal transformation through metamorphosis. It is a transition from the death of your old self into the birth of your new.

—Tom O'Connor, person with ARC

I never lost a game. I just ran out of time.

—Bobby Layne

Isn't it splendid to think of all the things there are to find out about? It just makes me feel glad to be alive—it's such an interesting world.

—Lucy Montgomery

Wake up with a smile and go after life.... Live it, enjoy it, taste it, smell it, feel it.

—Joe Knapp

I'm not overweight, I'm just nine inches too short.

—Shelley Winters

General Quotations About
Positive Thinking

The person who says it cannot be done
should not interrupt the person doing it.
—Chinese proverb

Being an optimist after you've got everything you want doesn't count.
—Kin Hubbard

There are more defects in temperament
than in the mind.
—Francois de La Rochefoucauld

Knock the "t" off the "can't."
—George Reeves

I make the most of all that comes and
the least of all that goes.
—Sara Teasdale

Clear your mind of "can't."
—Samuel Johnson

Rosiness is not a worse windowpane than gloomy gray when viewing the world.

—Grace Paley

One should ... be able to see things as hopeless and yet be determined to make them otherwise.

—F. Scott Fitzgerald

Doubt indulged soon becomes doubt realized.

—Francis Ridley Havergal

Do not sit long with a sad friend. When you go to a garden do you look at the weeds? Spend more time with the roses and jasmines.

—Jelaluddin Rumi

We have a problem. "Congratulations." But it's a tough problem. "Then double congratulations."

—W. Clement Stone

This I conceive to be the chemical function of humor: to change the character of our thought.

—Lin Yutang

It is never too late to be what you might have been.

—George Eliot

I will say this about being an optimist: even when things don't turn out well, you are certain they will get better.

—Frank Hughes

Whatever the ups and downs of detail within our limited experience, the larger whole is primarily beautiful.

—Gregory Bateson

People have a way of becoming what you encourage them to be—not what you nag them to be.

—S.N. Parker

Our self-image, strongly held, essentially determines what we become.
—Maxwell Maltz

To every disadvantage there is a corresponding advantage.
—W. Clement Stone

I learned really to practice mustard seed faith, and positive thinking, and remarkable things happened.
—Sir John Walton

Success produces success, just as money produces money.
—Nicolas de Chamfort

Failure is impossible.
—Susan B. Anthony

The only prison we need to escape from is the prison of our own minds.
—Anon.

He was a "how" thinker, not an "if" thinker.

—Anon.

Once you begin to believe there is help "out there," you will know it to be true.

—Saint Bartholomew

The quality of our expectations determines the quality of our actions.

—André Godin

The young do not know enough to be prudent, and therefore they attempt the impossible—and achieve it, generation after generation.

—Pearl S. Buck

What we love, we shall grow to resemble.

—Bernard of Clairvaux

No man can think clearly when his fists are clenched.

—George Jean Nathan

It is by sitting down to write every morning that he becomes a writer. Those who
do not do this remain amateurs.
                              —Gerald Brenan

Skill to do comes of doing.
                      —Ralph Waldo Emerson

How much shall I be changed, before I
am changed!
                              —John Donnell

We think in generalities, but we live in
detail.
                      —Alfred North Whitehead

There is no miraculous change that takes
place in a boy that makes him a man. He
becomes a man by being a man.
                              —Louis L'Amour

Some folks think they are thinking when
they are only rearranging their prejudices.
                              —Anon.

How things look on the outside of us
depends on how things are on the inside
of us.

—Park Cousins

The more we do, the more we can do;
the more busy we are, the more leisure
we have.

—William Hazlitt

In the end, the love you take is equal to
the love you make.

—Song lyric, "Abbey Road,"
Paul McCartney

PART FOUR

ENTHUSIASM

ENTHUSIASM IS ONE OF THE MOST IMPORTANT THINGS IN LIFE

Enthusiasm is life.

—Paul Scofield

Enthusiasm is the most important thing in life.

—Tennessee Williams

Enthusiasm signifies God in us.

—Madame de Stael

Life is enthusiasm, zest.

—Sir Lawrence Oliver

There is nothing greater than enthusiasm.

—Henry Moore

Enthusiasm is the most beautiful word on earth.

—Christian Morgenstern

Exuberance is beauty.

—William Blake

A man can be short and dumpy and getting bald but if he has fire, women will like him.

—Mae West

Most great men and women are not perfectly rounded in their personalties, but are instead people whose one driving enthusiasm is so great it makes their faults seem insignificant.

—Charles A. Cerami

What a man knows only through feeling can be explained only through enthusiasm.

—Joseph Joubert

What counts is not necessarily the size of the dog in the fight, but the size of the fight in the dog.

—Dwight D. Eisenhower

My enthusiasms ... constitute my reserves, my unexploited resources, perhaps my future.

—E.M. Cioran

In things pertaining to enthusiasm, no man is sane who does not know how to be insane on proper occasions.

—Henry Ward Beecher

Enthusiasm moves the world.

—J. Balfour

What hunger is in relation to food, zest is in relation to life.

—Bertrand Russell

Nothing is so contagious as enthusiasm; it moves stones, it charms brutes. Enthusiasm is the genius of sincerity, and truth accomplishes no victories without it.

—Edward Bulwer-Lytton

Winning isn't everything. Wanting to
win is.

—Catfish Hunter

Vitality! That's the pursuit of life, isn't it?
—Katharine Hepburn

All we need to make us really happy is
something to be enthusiastic about.
—Charles Kingsley

The great man is he who does not lose
his childlike heart.

—Mencius

Zest is the secret of all beauty. There is
no beauty that is attractive without zest.
—Christian Dior

What one has, one ought to use; and
whatever he does, he should do with all
his might.

—Cicero

Let us go singing as far as we go; the
road will be less tedious.

—Virgil

And whatsoever ye do, do it heartily.
—Col. 3:23

You will do foolish things, but do them
with enthusiasm.

—Colette

Whatever you attempt, go at it with
spirit. Put some in!
—David Starr Jordan

Nothing great was ever achieved without
enthusiasm.

—Ralph Waldo Emerson

Enthusiasm is nothing more or less than
faith in action.

—Henry Chester

Passion Is a Vital Force

Every man without passions has within him no principle of action, nor motive to act.

—Claude Helvetius

If we resist our passions, it is more from their weakness than from our strength.

—Francois de La Rochefoucauld

Without passion man is a mere latent force and possibility, like the flint which awaits the shock of the iron before it can give forth its spark.

—Henri Frederic Amiel

What is man but his passion?

—Robert Penn Warren

Only passions, great passions, can elevate the soul to great things.

—Denis Diderot

Nothing great in the world has been
accomplished without passion.

—George Hegel

Human nature, if it healthy, demands
excitement; and if it does not obtain its
thrilling excitement in the right way, it
will seek it in the wrong. God never
makes bloodless stoics; He makes no pas-
sionless saints.

—Oswald Chambers

All passions exaggerate; it is because they
do that they are passions.

—Nicolas de Chamfort

Be still when you have nothing to say;
when genuine passion moves you, say
what you've got to say, and say it hot.

—D.H. Lawrence

The passions are the only orators which
always persuade.

—Francois de La Rochefoucauld

This, indeed, is one of the eternal para-
doxes of both life and literature—that
without passion little gets done; yet,
without control of that passion, its effects
are largely ill or null.

—F.L. Lucas

Passion, though a bad regulator, is a powerful spring.

—Ralph Waldo Emerson

Our passions are ourselves.

—Anatole France

People who never get carried away
should be.

—Malcolm Forbes

A strong passion for any object will
ensure success, for the desire of the end
will point out the means.

—William Hazlitt

ENTHUSIASM MUST BE CHANNELED

The world belongs to the enthusiast who
keeps cool.

—William McFee

Optimism, unaccompanied by personal
effort, is merely a state of mind and not
fruitful.

—Edward L. Curtis

When enthusiasm is inspired by reason;
controlled by caution; sound in theory;
practical in application; reflects confidence; spreads good cheer; raises morale;
inspires associates; arouses loyalty; and
laughs at adversity, it is beyond price.

—Coleman Cox

Unless you give yourself to some great
cause, you haven't even begun to live.

—William P. Merrill

ENTHUSIASM AND WORK

If you aren't fired with enthusiasm, you will be fired with enthusiasm.

—Vince Lombardi

When his enthusiasm goes, he's through as a player.

—Pete Rose

Every production of genius must be the production of enthusiasm.

—Benjamin Disraeli

Give me a man who sings at his work.

—Thomas Carlyle

Enthusiasm for one's goal to lessens the disagreeableness of working toward it.

—Thomas Eakins

I rate enthusiasm even above professional skill.

—Sir Edward Appleton

ENTHUSIASM AND SUCCESS

Success is going from failure to failure
without loss of enthusiasm.

—Sir Winston Churchill

A man can succeed at almost anything
for which he has unlimited enthusiasm.

—Charles M. Schwab

Many of the most successful men I have
known have never grown up. They have
retained bubbling-over boyishness. They
have relished wit, they have indulged in
humor. They have not allowed "dignity"
to depress them into moroseness.
Youthfulness of spirit is the twin brother
of optimism, and optimism is the stuff of
which American business success is fash-
ioned. Resist growing up!

—B.C. Forbes

The world belongs to the energetic.

—Ralph Waldo Emerson

To bring one's self to a frame of mind and to the proper energy to accomplish things that require plain hard work continuously is the one big battle that everyone has. When this battle is won for all time, then everything is easy.

—Thomas A. Buckner

Faith that the thing can be done is essential to any great achievement.

—Thomas N. Carruther

If you have the will to win, you have achieved half your success; if you don't, you have achieved half your failure.

—David V.A. Ambrose

The real difference between men is energy.

—Thomas Fuller

Flaming enthusiasm, backed up by horse sense and persistence, is the quality that most frequently makes for success.

—Dale Carnegie

Optimism is essential to achievement
and it is also the foundation of courage
and of true progress.
—Nicholas Murray Butler

There is a passion for perfection which
you rarely see fully developed, but ... in
successful lives it is never wholly lacking.
—Bliss Carman

Sometimes success is due less to ability
than to zeal.
—Charles Buxton

Someone's always saying, "It's not
whether you win or lose," but if you feel
that way, you're as good as dead.
—James Caan

We would accomplish many more
things if we did not think of them as
impossible.
—C. Malesherbez

We can accomplish almost anything
within our ability if we but think that
we can!

—George Matthew Adams

Success is due less to ability than to zeal.

—Charles Buxton

He did it with all his heart, and prospered.

—2 Chr. 31:21

The real secret of success is enthusiasm.
Yes, more than enthusiasm, I would say
excitement. I like to see men get excited.
When they get excited they make a success of their lives.

—Walter Chrysler

Always bear in mind that your own resolution to success is more important than
any other one thing.

—Abraham Lincoln

The measure of an enthusiasm must be taken between interesting events. It is between bites that the lukewarm angler loses heart.

—Edwin Way Teale

To burn always with this hard gem-like flame. To maintain this ecstasy, is success in life.

—Walter Pater

The method of the enterprising is to plan with audacity and execute with vigor.

—Christian Bovee

Do it big or stay in bed.

—Larry Kelly

Every man is enthusiastic at times. One man has enthusiasm for thirty minutes, another man has it for thirty days. But it is the man who has it for thirty years who makes a success in life.

—Edward B. Butler

It is the greatest shot of adrenaline to be doing what you've wanted to do so badly. You almost feel like you could fly without the plane.

—Charles Lindbergh

What a man accomplishes in a day depends upon the way in which he approaches his tasks. When we accept tough jobs as a challenge to our ability and wade into them with joy and enthusiasm, miracles can happen. When we do our work with a dynamic, conquering spirit, we get things done.

—Arland Gilbert

If you're not happy every morning when you get up, leave for work, or start to work at home—if you're not enthusiastic about doing that, you're not going to be successful.

—Donald M. Kendall

ENTHUSIASM AND KNOWLEDGE

Zeal will do more than knowledge.
—William Hazlitt

Let a man in a garret burn with enough
intensity, and he will set fire to the
world.
—Antoine de Saint-Exupery

Knowledge is power, but enthusiasm
pulls the switch.
—Ivern Ball

Through zeal, knowledge is gotten;
through lack of zeal, knowledge is lost.
—Buddha

I prefer the errors of enthusiasm to the
indifference of wisdom.
—Anatole France

Enthusiasm and Energy

Energy will do anything that can be done
in this world.

—Johann von Goethe

The difference between one man and
another is not mere ability ... it is energy.

—Thomas Arnold

Energy, even like the Biblical grain of
mustard-seed, will move mountains.

—Hosea Ballou

I studied the lives of great men and
famous women, and I found that the
men and women who got to the top were
those who did the jobs they had in hand,
with everything they had of energy and
enthusiasm and hard work.

—Harry S. Truman

The only thing that keeps a man going is energy. And what is energy but liking life?

—Louis Auchincloss

Energy and persistence conquer all things.

—Benjamin Franklin

The will to conquer is the first condition of victory.

—Marshal Ferdinand Foch

You see me in my most virile moment when you see me doing what I do. When I am directing, a special energy comes upon me.... It is only when I am doing my work that I feel truly alive. It is like having sex.

—Federico Fellini

Man never rises to great truths without enthusiasm.

—Vauvenargues

ENTHUSIASM AND AGE

No one grows old by living, only by losing interest in living.
>—Marie Beynon Ray

None are so old as those who have outlived enthusiasm.
>—Henry David Thoreau

It is energy, the central element of which is will, that produces the miracles of enthusiasm in all ages. It is the mainspring of force of character and the sustaining power of all great action.
>—Samuel Smiles

Years wrinkle the face, but to give up enthusiasm wrinkles the soul.
>—Watterson Lowe

Pleasure is the only thing to live for. Nothing ages like happiness.
>—Oscar Wilde

ENTHUSIASM AND WARFARE

He fights with spirit as well as with the sword.

—Latin proverb

It is fatal to enter any war without the will to win it.

—General Douglas MacArthur

Morale is the greatest single factor in successful wars.

—Dwight D. Eisenhower

The aim of military training is not just to prepare men for battle, but to make them long for it.

—Louis Simpson

Wars may be fought with weapons, but they are won by men. It is the spirit of men who follow and of the man who leads that gains the victory.

—General George S. Patton

Primary Sources of Enthusiasm

Enthusiasm can only be aroused by two things: first, an ideal which takes the imagination by storm, and second, a definite, intelligible plan for carrying that ideal into practice.

—Arnold Toynbee

No one keeps up his enthusiasm automatically. Enthusiasm must be nourished with new actions, new aspirations, new efforts, new vision. Compete with yourself; set your teeth and dive into the job of breaking your own record. It is one's own fault if his enthusiasm is gone; he has failed to feed it.

—Papyrus

The same reason makes a man a religious enthusiast that makes a man an enthusiast in any other way ... an uncomfortable mind in an uncomfortable body.

—William Hazlitt

The great composer does not set to work because he is inspired, but becomes inspired because he is working. Beethoven, Wagner, Bach and Mozart settled down day after day to the job in hand with as much regularity as an accountant settles down each day to his figures. They didn't waste time waiting for inspiration.

—Ernest Newman

Practice being excited.

—Bill Foster

Opposition inflames the enthusiast, never converts him.

—J.C.F. von Schiller

Whatever course you have chosen for yourself, it will not be a chore but an adventure if you bring to it a sense of the glory of striving, if your sights are set far above the merely secure and mediocre.

—David Sarnoff

Earnestness and sincereness are synony-
mous.

—Corita Kent

Vigor is contagious, and whatever makes
us either think or feel strongly adds to
our power and enlarges our field of
action.

—Ralph Waldo Emerson

Man never rises to great truths without
enthusiasm.

—Vauvenargues

Reason alone is insufficient to make us
enthusiastic in any matter.

—Francois de La Rochefoucauld

PART FIVE

ROLE MODELS

THE RIGHT ROLE MODEL CAN BE
VERY INSPIRATIONAL

To be ignorant of the lives of the most
celebrated men of antiquity is to continue in a state of childhood.

—Plutarch

As it is our nature to be more moved by
hope than fear, the example of one we
see abundantly rewarded cheers and
encourages us far more than the sight of
many who have not been well treated
disquiets us.

—Francesco Guicciardini

Nothing arouses ambition so much as
the trumpet clang of another's fame.

—Baltasar Gracian

People never improve unless they look to
some standard or example higher and
better than themselves.

—Tyron Edwards

Keep away from people who try to belittle your ambitions. Small people always do that, but the really great make you feel that you, too, can become great.

—Mark Twain

Without heroes, we are all plain people, and don't know how far we can go.

—Bernard Malamud

That some should be rich shows that others may become rich, and hence is just encouragement to industry and enterprise.

—Abraham Lincoln

The best teachers of humanity are the lives of great men.

—Charles H. Fowler

People seldom improve when they have no other model but themselves to copy.

—Oliver Goldsmith

As you get older it is harder to have heroes, but it is sort of necessary.
—Ernest Hemingway

Lives of great men all remind us we can make our lives sublime; and, departing, leave behind us, footprints on the sands of time.
—Henry Wadsworth Longfellow

Very few men are wise by their own counsel, or learned by their own teaching. For he that was only taught by himself had a fool for his master.
—Ben Johnson

Call the roll in your memory of conspicuously successful business giants and ... you will be struck by the fact that almost every one of them encountered inordinate difficulties sufficient to crush all but the gamest of spirits. Edison went hungry many times before he became famous.
—B.C. Forbes

WE ALL NEED GOOD EXAMPLES

A good example is the best sermon.
—Anon.

Example has more followers than reason.
—Christian Bovee

Example is the school of mankind, and
they will learn at no other.
—Burke

The most important single influence in
the life of a person is another person ...
who is worthy of emulation.
—Paul D. Shafer

One filled with joy preaches without
preaching.
—Mother Teresa

Example is not the main thing in influ-
encing others. It is the only thing.
—Albert Schweitzer

Judgement can be acquired only by acute observation, by actual experience in the school of life, by ceaseless alertness to learn from others, by study of the activities of men who have made notable marks, by striving to analyze the everyday play of causes and effects, by constant study of human nature.

—B.C. Forbes

Example moves the world more than doctrine.

—Henry Miller

Nothing is so infectious as example.

—Francois de La Rochefoucauld

If ... you can't be a good example, then you'll just have to be a horrible warning.

—Catherine Aird

Is there anyone so wise as to learn by the experience of others?

—Voltaire

IMITATION

There is a difference between imitating a
good man and counterfeiting him.
—Benjamin Franklin

Each of us is in fact what he is almost
exclusively by virtue of his imitativeness.
—William James

Imitation is a necessity of human nature.
—Oliver Wendell Holmes, Jr.

When people are free to do as they
please, they usually imitate each other.
—Eric Hoffer

'Tis no shame to follow the better prece-
dent.
—Ben Johnson

Emulation is a noble and just passion,
full of appreciation.
—J.C.F. von Schiller

Men, like nails, lose their usefulness
when they lose direction and begin to
bend.

—Walter Savage Landor

Emulation admires and strives to imitate
great actions; envy is only moved to
malice.

—Honore de Balzac

Imitation can acquire pretty much everything but the power which created the
thing imitated.

—Henry S. Haskins

Almost all absurdity of conduct arises
from the imitation of those whom we
cannot resemble.

—Samuel Johnson

A prudent person profits from personal
experience, a wise one from the experience of others.

—Dr. Joseph Collins

LEARNING FROM OTHERS' MISTAKES

From the errors of others, a wise man corrects his own.

—Publilius Syrus

Learn from the mistakes of others—you can't live long enough to make them all yourself.

—Martin Vanbee

Wise men learn by other men's mistakes, fools by their own.

—H.G. Bohn

A man is fortunate if he encounters living examples of vice, as well as of virtue, to inspire him.

—Brendan Francis

Learn to see in another's calamity the ills which you should avoid.

—Publilius Syrus

PART SIX

GOALS

It's Tremendously Important to Have Good Goals

An aim in life is the only fortune worth finding.
> —Jacqueline Kennedy Onassis

Purpose is what gives life a meaning.
> —C.H. Parkhurst

He is conscious of touching the highest pinnacle of fulfillment ... when he is consumed in the service of an idea, in the conquest of the goal pursued.
> —R. Briffault

The great and glorious masterpiece of man is to know how to live to purpose.
> —Michel de Montaigne

You have to have a dream so you can get up in the morning.
> —Billy Wilder

The tragedy of life doesn't lie in not reaching your goal. The tragedy lies in having no goal to reach.

—Benjamin Mays

The poor man is not he who is without a cent, but he who is without a dream.

—Harry Kemp

He who has a why to live for can bear almost any how.

—Friedrich Nietzsche

Great minds have purposes, others have wishes.

—Washington Irving

Be a life long or short, its completeness depends on what it was lived for.

—David Starr Jordan

The true worth of a man is to be measured by the objects he pursues.

—Marcus Aurelius

To live means to have ... a mission to fulfill—and in the measure in which we avoid setting our life to something, we make it empty.

—José Ortega y Gasset

To seek one's goals and to drive toward it, steeling one's heart, is most uplifting!

—Henrik Ibsen

A useless life is an early death.

—Johann von Goethe

My father used to play with my brother and me in the yard. Mother would come out and say, "You're tearing up the grass." "We're not raising grass," Dad would reply. "We're raising boys."

—Harmon Killebrew

Without a purpose, nothing should be done.

—Marcus Aurelius

Our plans miscarry because they have no aim. When a man does not know what harbor he is making for, no wind is the right wind.

—Marcus Annaeus Seneca

Every true man, sir, who is a little above the level of the beasts and plants, lives so as to give a meaning and a value to his own life.

—Luigi Pirandello

Men cannot for long live hopefully unless they are embarked upon some great unifying enterprise, one for which they may pledge their lives, their fortunes and their honor.

—C.A. Dykstra

No pleasure philosophy, no sensuality, no place nor power, no material success can for a moment give such inner satisfaction as the sense of living for good purpose.

—Minot Simons

Many are stubborn in pursuit of the path they have chosen, few in pursuit of the goal.

—Friedrich Nietzsche

There is one thing which gives radiance to everything. It is the idea of something around the corner.

—G.K. Chesterton

Lack of something to feel important about is almost the greatest tragedy a man may have.

—Charles C. Noble

There are three ingredients in the good life: learning, earning and yearning.

—Christopher Morely

To grow and know what one is growing towards—that is the source of all strength and confidence in life.

—James Baillie

If you cry "Forward," you must make
plain in what direction to go.
                    —Anton Chekov

In everything one must consider the end.
                    —Jean de La Fontaine

A novelist must know what his last chapter is going to say and one way or
another work toward that last chapter....
To me it is utterly basic, yet it seems like
it's a great secret.
                    —Leon Uris

The purpose of life is a life of purpose.
                    —Robert Byrne

Life has a value only when it has something valuable as its object.
                    —George Hegel

Obstacles are those frightful things you
see when you take your eyes off the goal.
                    —Hannah More

You must have long-range goals to keep you from being frustrated by short-range failures.

—Charles C. Noble

The world stands aside to let anyone pass who knows where he is going.

—David Starr Jordan

It is when things go hardest, when life becomes most trying, that there is greatest need for having a fixed goal. When few comforts come from without, it is all the more necessary to have a fount to draw on from within.

—B.C. Forbes

Having a goal is a state of happiness.

—E.J. Bartek

There's some end at last for the man who follows a path; mere rambling is interminable.

—Marcus Annaeus Seneca

An aspiration is a joy forever, a possession as solid as a landed estate, a fortune which we can never exhaust and which gives us year by year a revenue of pleasurable activity.

      —Robert Louis Stevenson

A straight path never leads anywhere except to the objective.

      —André Gide

This is true joy of life—the being used for a purpose that is recognized by yourself as a right one, instead of being a feverish, selfish little clod of ailments and grievances, complaining that the world will not devote itself to making you happy.

      —George Bernard Shaw

Not only must we be good, but we must also be good for something.

      —Henry David Thoreau

The American people can have anything they want; the trouble is, they don't know what they want.

—Eugene V. Debs

Life has a meaning only if one barters it day by day for something other than itself.

—Antoine de Saint-Exupery

To have a reason to get up in the morning, it is necessary to possess a guiding principle. A belief of some kind. A bumper sticker, if you will.

—Judith Guest

The soul that has no established aim loses itself.

—Michel de Montaigne

He turns not back who is bound to a star.

—Leonardo da Vinci

To have no set purpose in one's life is the harlotry of the will.

—Stephen McKenna

There is no happiness except in the realization that we have accomplished something.

—Henry Ford

He might never really do what he said, but at least he had it in mind. He had somewhere to go.

—Louis L'Amour

Set short term goals and you'll win games. Set long term goals and you'll win championships!

—Anon.

Laboring toward distant aims sets the mind in a higher key, and puts us at our best.

—C.H. Parkhurst

The great and glorious masterpiece of
man is how to live with a purpose.
—Michel de Montaigne

Everything's in the mind. That's where it
all starts. Knowing what you want is the
first step toward getting it.
—Mae West

Happiness is the overcoming of not
unknown obstacles toward a known goal.
—L. Ron Hubbard

Strong lives are motivated by dynamic
purposes.
—Kenneth Hildebrand

What most counts is not to live, but to
live aright.
—Socrates

The purpose of life is life.
—Karl Lagerfeld

Having a dream isn't stupid.... It's not
having a dream that's stupid.

—Anon.

Choosing a goal and sticking to it
changes everything.

—Scott Reed

No wind serves him who addresses his
voyage to no certain port.

—Michel de Montaigne

We act as though comfort and luxury
were the chief requirements of life, when
all that we need to make us really happy
is something to be enthusiastic about.

—Charles Kingsley

Aim at nothing and you'll succeed.

—Anon.

Unhappiness is in not knowing what we
want and killing ourselves to get it.

—Don Herold

One of the sources of pride in being a human being is the ability to bear present frustrations in the interests of longer purposes.

—Helen Merrell Lynd

Destiny is not a matter of chance, it is a matter of choice; it is not a thing to be waited for, it is a thing to be achieved.

—William Jennings Bryan

Where no plan is laid, where the disposal of time is surrendered merely to the chance of incident, chaos will soon reign.

—Victor Hugo

Only he who can see the invisible can do the impossible.

—Frank Gaines

If you don't know where you are going, how can you expect to get there?

—Basil S. Walsh

The only people who attain power are those who crave for it.

—Erich Kastner

Nothing is more terrible than activity without insight.

—Thomas Carlyle

In this life we get only those things for which we hunt, for which we strive, and for which we are willing to sacrifice.

—George Matthew Adams

You seldom get what you go after unless you know in advance what you want.

—Maurice Switzer

A life that hasn't a definite plan is likely to become driftwood.

—David Sarnoff

Only he who keeps his eye fixed on the far horizon will find his right road.

—Dag Hammarskjold

We Each Have Our Own Goals

Every man is said to have his peculiar
ambition.

—Abraham Lincoln

If we would only give, just once, the
same amount of reflection to what we
want to get out of life that we give to the
question of what to do with a two weeks'
vacation, we would be startled at our
false standards and the aimless procession
of our busy days.

—Dorothy Canfield Fisher

We all live with the objective of being
happy; our lives are all different, and yet
the same.

—Anne Frank

Follow your bliss. Find where it is and
don't be afraid to follow it.

—Joseph Campbell

I am not sending messages with my feet.
All I ever wanted was not to come up
empty. I did it for the dough, and the
old applause.

—Fred Astaire

First say to yourself what you would be,
and then do what you have to do.

—Epictetus

We can do whatever we wish to do pro-
vided our wish is strong enough.... What
do you want most to do? That's what I
have to keep asking myself, in the face of
difficulties.

—Katherine Mansfield

The aim of life is self-development, to
realize one's nature perfectly.

—Oscar Wilde

Enthusiasm for one's goal lessens the disagreeableness of working toward it.

—Thomas Eakins

To be what we are, and to become what we are capable of becoming, is the only end of life.

—Baruch Spinoza

Ambition means longing and striving to attain some purpose. Therefore, there are as many brands of ambition as there are human aspirations.

—B.C. Forbes

Fortunate is the person who has developed the self-control to steer a straight course toward his objective in life, without being swayed from his purpose by either commendation or condemnation.

—Napoleon Hill

Concentrate on finding your goal, then concentrate on reaching it.

—Colonel Michael Friedman

WE CAN HAVE TOO MANY GOALS

He who wants to do everything will
never do anything.

—André Maurois

As you emphasize your life, you must
localize and define it ... you cannot do
everything.

—Phillips Brooks

There are people who want to be everywhere at once, and they get nowhere.

—Carl Sandburg

Nations, like individuals, have to limit
their objectives or take the consequences.

—James Reston

A windmill is eternally at work to accomplish one end, although it shifts with
every variation of the weathercock, and
assumes ten different positions in a day.

—Charles Caleb Colton

People can have many different kinds of
pleasure. The real one is that for which
they will forsake the others.

—Marcel Proust

I can tell you how to get what you want:
You've just got to keep a thing in view
and go for it and never let your eyes
wander to right or left or up or down.
And looking back is fatal.

—William J. Lock

One of the most important factors, not
only in military matters but in life as a
whole, is ... the ability to direct one's
whole energies towards the fulfillment of
a particular task.

—Field Marshal Erwin Rommel

One cannot manage too many affairs:
like pumpkins in the water, one pops up
while you try to hold down the other.

—Chinese proverb

It is in self-limitation that a master first
shows himself.

> —Johann von Goethe

One principle reason why men are so
often useless is that they ... divide and
shift their attention among a multitude
of objects and pursuits.

> —Nathaniel Emmons

A bull does not enjoy fame in two herds.

> —Rhodesian proverb

He who begins many things finishes but
few.

> —Italian proverb

Who begins too much accomplishes little.

> —German proverb

Never try to catch two frogs with one
hand.

> —Chinese proverb

If you run after two hares, you will catch neither.

—Thomas Fuller

The greyhound that starts many hares kills none.

—Spanish proverb

No man can serve two masters: for either he will hate the one, and love the other; or else he will hold to the one, and despise the other.

— Mt. 6:24

He who serves two masters has to lie to one.

—Portuguese proverb

Those who attain any excellence commonly spend life in one pursuit; for excellence is not often granted upon easier terms.

—Samuel Johnson

He who wishes to fulfill his mission in the world must be a man of one idea, one great overmastering purpose, overshadowing all his aims, and guiding and controlling his entire life.

—Bate

Firmness of purpose is one of the most necessary sinews of character and one of the best instruments of success. Without it, genius wastes its efforts in a maze of inconsistencies.

—Lord Chesterfield

A double-minded man is unstable in all his ways.... A determinate purpose in life, and a steady adhesion to it through all disadvantages, are indispensable conditions of success.

—William M. Punshion

He who hunts two hares leaves one and loses the other.

—Japanese proverb

If you would be Pope, you must think of nothing else.

—Spanish proverb

One should want only one thing and want it constantly. Then one is sure of getting it. But I desire everything, and consequently get nothing.

—André Gide

I take it as a prime cause of the present confusion of society that it is too sickly and too doubtful to use pleasure as a test of value.

—Rebecca West

I care not what your education is, elaborate or nothing, what your mental calibre is, great or small, that man who concentrates all his energies of body, mind and soul in one direction is a tremendous man.

—T. DeWitt Talmage

MAKE THE ENJOYMENT OF LIFE
A PRIMARY GOAL

All animals except man know that the
ultimate of life is to enjoy it.

—Samuel Butler

The goal of all civilization, all religious
thought, and all that sort of thing is simply to have a good time. But man gets so
solemn over the process that he forgets
the end.

—Don Marquis

Let us live, while we are alive!

—Johann von Goethe

Since we must all die sooner or later, let
us enjoy life while we can!

—Otoma no Tabito

Life is about enjoying yourself and having a good time.

—Cher

Life is an end in itself, and the only question as to whether it is worth living is whether you have had enough of it.
—Oliver Wendell Holmes, Jr.

There is no cure for birth and death save to enjoy the interval.
—George Santayana

I finally figured out the only reason to be alive is to enjoy it.
—Rita Mae Brown

All men seek one goal: success or happiness.
—Aristotle

The business of life is to enjoy oneself; everything else is a mockery.
—Norman Douglas

There is only one meaning of life: the act of living itself.
—Erich Fromm

The true object of human life is play.
—G.K. Chesterton

Use your health, even to the point of
wearing it out. That is what it is for.
Spend all you have before you die; do
not outlive yourself.
—George Bernard Shaw

Pleasure is the object, duty and the goal
of all rational creatures.
—Voltaire

Life exists for the love of music or beautiful things.
—G.K. Chesterton

The main obligation is to amuse yourself.
—S.J. Perelman

The very first condition of lasting happiness is that a life should be full of purpose, aiming at something outside self.
—Hugh Black

GOALS AND PEACE OF MIND

From his cradle to the grave, a man never does a single thing which has any first and foremost object save one—to secure peace of mind, spiritual comfort, for himself.

—Mark Twain

I take it that what all men are really after is some form of, perhaps only some formula of, peace.

—James Conrad

I am searching for that which every man seeks—peace and rest.

—Dante Alighieri

The full-grown modern human being ... is conscious of touching the highest pinnacle of fulfillment ... when he is consumed in the service of an idea, in the conquest of the goal pursued.

—R. Briffault

ALWAYS AIM HIGH

Why should I deem myself to be a chisel,
when I could be the artist?
                    —J.C.F. von Schiller

Once you say you're going to settle for
second, that's what happens to you.
                    —John F. Kennedy

Aim at heaven and you get earth thrown
in; aim at earth and you get neither.
                    —C.S. Lewis

When you reach for the stars, you may
not quite get one, but you won't come
up with a handful of mud, either.
                    —Leo Burnett

In the long run men hit only what they
aim at. Therefore, though they should
fall immediately, they had better aim at
something high.
                    —Henry David Thoreau

Aim at the sun, and you may not reach
it; but your arrow will fly far higher
than if aimed at an object on a level
with yourself.

—J. Hawes

The most absurd and reckless aspirations
have sometimes led to extraordinary success.

—Vauvenargues

If you would hit the mark, you must aim
a little above it; every arrow that flies
feels the attraction of earth.

—Henry Wadsworth Longfellow

Unless in one thing or another we are
straining toward perfection, we have for-
feited our manhood.

—Stephen McKenna

Man's reach should exceed his grasp, or
what's a heaven for?

—Robert Browning

The tragedy of life doesn't lie in not reaching your goal. The tragedy lies in having no goal to reach. It isn't a calamity to die with dreams unfulfilled, but it is a calamity not to dream. It is not disgrace to reach the stars, but it is a disgrace to have no stars to reach for. Not failure, but low aim, is a sin.

—Benjamin Mays

Too low they build, who build beneath the stars.

—Edward Young

Whatever course you have chosen for yourself, it will not be a chore but an adventure if you bring to it a sense of the glory of striving, if your sights are set far above the merely secure and mediocre.

—David Sarnoff

We are all in the gutter, but some of us are looking at the stars.

—Oscar Wilde

Aim at perfection in everything, though in most things it is unattainable. However they who aim at it, and persevere, will come much nearer to it than those whose laziness and despondency make them give it up as unattainable.

—Lord Chesterfield

A man's worth is no greater than the worth of his ambitions.

—Marcus Aurelius

One may miss the mark by aiming too high, as too low.

—Thomas Fuller

Shoot for the moon. Even if you miss it, you will land among the stars.

—Les Brown

We aim above the mark to hit the mark. Every act hath some falsehood or exaggeration in it.

—Ralph Waldo Emerson

Life is a petty thing unless it is moved by the indomitable urge to extend its boundaries.

—José Ortega y Gasset

Far away in the sunshine are my highest inspirations. I many not reach them, but I can look up and see the beauty, believe in them and try to follow where they lead.

—Louisa May Alcott

Not failure, but low aim, is crime.

—James Russell Lowell

Great is the road I climb, but ... the garland offered by an easier effort is not worth the gathering.

—Propertius

I never took a position we were going to be a good ball club. I took the position we were going to be a winning ball club.

—Red Auerbach

Before you begin a thing, remind yourself that difficulties and delays quite impossible to foresee are ahead.... You can only see one thing clearly and that is your goal. Form a mental vision of that and cling to it through thick and thin.

—Kathleen Norris

If one advances confidently in the direction of his dreams, and endeavors to live the life which he has imagined, he will meet with a success unexpected in common hours.

—Henry David Thoreau

Man can only receive what he sees himself receiving.

—Florence Scovel Shinn

A person can grow only as much as his horizon allows.

—John Powell

GOALS AND HAPPINESS

Enjoyment is not a goal, it is a feeling
that accompanies important ongoing
activity.

—Paul Goodman

What our deepest self craves is not mere
enjoyment, but some supreme purpose
that will enlist all our powers and give
unity and direction to our life.

—Henry J. Golding

The only true happiness comes from
squandering ourselves for a purpose.

—John Mason Brown

There is more to life than just existing
and having a pleasant time.

—J.C.F. von Schiller

Happiness is not the end of life; character is.

—Henry Ward Beecher

Many persons have a wrong idea of what constitutes true happiness. It is not attained through self-gratification, but through fidelity to a worthy purpose.

—Helen Keller

There is no happiness except in the realization that we have accomplished something.

—Henry Ford

Having a goal is a state of happiness.

—E.J. Bartek

Happiness is essentially a state of going somewhere, wholeheartedly, one-directionally, without regret or reservation.

—William H. Sheldon

Happiness lies in the joy of achievement and the thrill of creative effort.

—Franklin Delano Roosevelt

DOING OUR DUTY AND PURSUING GOALS LEADS TO HAPPINESS

This is true joy of life—being used for a purpose that is recognized by yourself as a mighty one ... instead of being a feverish, selfish little clod of ailments and grievances, complaining that the world will not devote itself to making you happy.

—George Bernard Shaw

Never mind your happiness; do your duty.

—Will Durant

Human happiness and moral duty are inseparably connected.

—George Washington

When we ... devote ourselves to the strict and unsparing performance of duty, then happiness comes of itself.

—Wilhelm von Humboldt

Seek happiness for its own sake, and you will not find it; seek for duty, and happiness will follow, as the shadow comes with the sunshine.

—Tyron Edwards

The secret of living is to find ... the pivot of a concept on which you can make your stand.

—Luigi Pirandello

The only true happiness comes from squandering ourselves for a purpose.

—William Cowper

True happiness, we are told, consists in getting out of one's self, but the point is not only to get out; you must stay out, and to stay out, you must have some absorbing errand.

—Henry James

Happiness is the natural flower of duty.

—Phillips Brooks

The happiest excitement in life is to be convinced that one is fighting for all one is worth on behalf of some clearly seen and deeply felt good.

—Ruth Benedict

The man who fails because he aims astray, or because he does not aim at all, is to be found everywhere.

—Frank Swinnerton

Happy the man who knows his duties!
—Christian Furchtegott Gellert

The object of war is not to die for your country, but to make the other bastard die for his.

—General George S. Patton

He who never sacrificed a present to a future good, or a personal to a general one, can speak of happiness only as the blind speak of color.

—Horace Mann

Happy the man who knows his duties!
        —Christian Furchtegott Gellert

I believe half the unhappiness in life
comes from people being afraid to go
straight at things.
        —William J. Locke

Happiness is the overcoming of not
unknown obstacles toward a known goal.
        —L. Ron Hubbard

The only ones among you who will be
really happy are those who will have
sought and found how to serve.
        —Albert Schweitzer

Give a man health and a course to steer,
and he'll never stop to trouble about
whether he's happy or not.
        —George Bernard Shaw

Without duty, life is soft and boneless.
        —Joseph Joubert

SUCCESS

The man who succeeds above his fellows is the one who early in life discerns his object and toward that object habitually directs his powers. Even genius itself is but fine observation strengthened by fixity of purpose.

—Edward Bulwer-Lytton

A determinate purpose of life, and steady adhesion to it through all disadvantages, are indispensable conditions of success.

—William M. Punshon

Life has ... taught me not to expect success to be the inevitable result of my endeavors. She taught me to seek sustenance from the endeavor itself, but to leave the result to God.

—Alan Paton

ULTIMATE GOALS

Much pleasure and little grief is every
man's desire.

—Spanish proverb

I think the purpose of life is to be useful,
to be responsible, to be honorable, to be
compassionate. It is, after all, to matter:
to count, to stand for something, to
have made some difference that you
lived at all.

—Leo C. Rosten

The great business of life is to be, to do,
to do without, and to depart.

—John Morley

The proper function of man is to live—
not to exist.

—Jack London

Life's objective is life itself.

—Johann von Goethe

I seek the utmost pleasure and the least pain.

—Plautus

There are two things to aim at in life: first, to get what you want, and after that to enjoy it. Only the wisest of mankind achieve the second.

—Logan Pearsall Smith

Reach high, for stars lie hidden in your soul. Dream deep, for every dream precedes the goal.

—Pamela Vaull Starr

Never undertake anything for which you wouldn't have the courage to ask the blessings of heaven.

—Georg Christoph Lichtenberg

The one thing worth living for is to keep one's soul pure.

—Marcus Aurelius

The greatest use of life is to spend it for something that will outlast it.

—William James

PART SEVEN

LOOKING AHEAD

WE'RE NOT SUPPOSED TO SEE
TOO FAR AHEAD

It is a mistake to look too far ahead.
Only one link in the chain of destiny can
be handled at a time.
> —Sir Winston Churchill

Neither in the life of the individual nor
in that of mankind is it desirable to
know the future.
> —Jakob Burckhardt

There is no data on the future.
> —Laurel Cutler

God made the world round so we
would never be able to see too far down
the road.
> —Isak Dinesen

The future comes one day at a time.
> —Dean Acheson

There is a case, and a strong case, for that particular form of indolence that allows us to move through life knowing only what immediately concerns us.
—Alec Waugh

Cease to inquire what the future has in store, and take as a gift whatever the day brings forth.
—Horace

The best thing about the future is that it comes only one day at a time.
—Abraham Lincoln

Hardly anyone knows how much is gained by ignoring the future.
—Bernard de Fontenelle

The future is hidden even from those who make it.
—Anatole France

Tomorrow's Always Another Day

They who lose today may win tomorrow.
—Miguel de Cervantes

Be of good cheer. Do not think of today's failures, but of the success that may come tomorrow. You have set yourselves a difficult task, but you will succeed if you persevere; and you will find a joy in overcoming obstacles. Remember, no effort that we make to attain something beautiful is ever lost.

—Helen Keller

I have been nothing ... but there is tomorrow.

—Louis L'Amour

After all, tomorrow is another day.
—Scarlett O'Hara,
Gone With The Wind

We Can't Be Afraid
of the Future

He who foresees calamities suffers them
twice over.

> —Beilby Porteous

Only man clogs his happiness with care,
destroying what is with thoughts of what
may be.

> —John Dryden

If you are afraid for your future, you
don't have a present.

> —James Petersen

He that fears not the future may enjoy
the present.

> —Thomas Fuller

Cowards die many times before their
deaths; the valiant never taste of death
but once.

> —William Shakespeare

The future is called "perhaps," which is the only possible thing to call the future. And the important thing is not to allow that to scare you.

—Tennessee Williams

I am not afraid of tomorrow, for I have seen yesterday and I love today.

—William Allen White

Go forth to meet the shadowy Future without fear and with a manly heart.

—Henry Wadsworth Longfellow

To relinquish a present good through apprehension of a future evil is in most instances unwise ... from a fear which may afterwards turn out groundless, you lost the good that lay within your grasp.

—Francesco Guicciardini

It is never safe to look into the future with eyes of fear.

—E.H. Harriman

Nothing in life is more remarkable than
the unnecessary anxiety which we
endure, and generally create ourselves.
                              —Benjamin Disraeli

Every tomorrow has two handles. We can
take hold of it with the handle of anxiety
or the handle of faith.
                              —Henry Ward Beecher

Every man, through fear, mugs his aspirations a dozen times a day.
                              —Brendan Francis

The mere apprehension of a coming evil
has put many into a situation of the
utmost danger.
                              —Lucan

We need not be afraid of the future, for
the future will be in our own hands.
                              —Thomas E. Dewey

WE MUST LEARN
TO TRUST THE FUTURE

When all else is lost, the future still
remains.

—Christian Bovee

Everyone has it within his power to say,
this I am today, that I shall be tomorrow.

—Louis L'Amour

Take therefore no thought of the morrow; for the morrow shall take thought
for the things of itself.

— Mt. 6:34

We grow in time to trust the future for
our answers.

—Ruth Benedict

Put aside the need to know some future
design and simply leave your life open to
what is needed of it by the Divine forces.

—Emmanuel

The only limit to our realization of tomorrow will be our doubts of today. Let us move forward with strong and active faith.

—Franklin Delano Roosevelt

Where will I be five years from now? I delight in not knowing. That's one of the greatest things about life—its wonderful surprises.

—Marlo Thomas

To persevere, trusting in what hopes he has, is courage. The coward despairs.

—Euripides

It is not the cares of today, but the cares of tomorrow, that weigh a man down. For the needs of today we have corresponding strength given. For the morrow we are told to trust. It is not ours yet.

—George MacDonald

OTHER DEFINITIONS OF TOMORROW AND THE FUTURE

Tomorrow is the day when idlers work,
and fools reform, and mortal men lay
hold on heaven.

—Edward Young

The future is the most expensive luxury
in the world.

—Thornton Wilder

Tomorrow is the mysterious, unknown
guest.

—Henry Wadsworth Longfellow

Tomorrow is the only day in the year
that appeals to a lazy man.

—Jimmy Lyons

The future is something which everyone
reaches at the rate of sixty minutes an
hour, whatever he does, whoever he is.

—C.S. Lewis

The future is a world limited by our-selves—in it we discover only what con-cerns us.

—Maurice Maeterlinck

The future is only the past again, entered through another gate.

—Arthur Wing Pinero

The future is the shape of things to come.

—H. G. Wells

The future is the past in preparation.

—Pierre Dac

To the being of fully alive, the future is not ominous but a promise; it surrounds the present like a halo.

—John Dewey

The future is hope!

—John Fiske

GENERAL QUOTATIONS ABOUT
TOMORROW AND THE FUTURE

Grow old along with me! The best is yet to be.

—Robert Browning

He who lives in the future lives in a featureless blank; he lives in impersonality; he lives in Nirvana. The past is democratic, because it is a people. The future is despotic, because it is a caprice. Every man is alone in his prediction, just as each man is alone in a dream.

—G.K. Chesterton

The future belongs to those who believe in the beauty of their dreams.

—Eleanor Roosevelt

I like the dreams of the future better than the history of the past.

—Thomas Jefferson

You cannot plan the future by the past.
—Edmund Burke

It is when tomorrow's burden is added to the burden of today that the weight is more than a man can bear.
—George MacDonald

My interest is in the future because I am going to spend the rest of my life there.
—Charles F. Kettering

I never think of the future. It comes soon enough.
—Albert Einstein

Yesterday is not ours to recover, but tomorrow is ours to win or lose.
—Lyndon B. Johnson

The possibilities for tomorrow are usually beyond our expectations.
—Anon.

The future is a great land.

—Anon.

The future is wider than vision, and has no end.

—Donald G. Mitchell

When I look at the future, it's so bright, it burns my eyes.

—Oprah Winfrey

Everyone's future is, in reality, uncertain and full of unknown treasures from which all may draw unguessed prizes.

—Lord Dunsany

The future is made of the same stuff as the present.

—Simone Weil

The future is much like the present, only longer.

—Dan Quisenberry

The bridges you cross before you come
to them are over rivers that aren't there.
—Gene Brown

Fortunately for children, the uncertain-
ties of the present always give way to the
enchanted possibilities of the future.
—Gelsey Kirkland

I left off and made some marmalade. It's
amazing how it cheers one up to shred
oranges and scrub the floor.
—D.H. Lawrence

For you and me, today is all we have;
tomorrow is a mirage that may never
become reality.
—Louis L'Amour

If a man carefully examines his thoughts
he will be surprised to find how much he
lives in the future. His well-being is
always ahead.
—Ralph Waldo Emerson

By-and-by never comes.
>   —Saint Augustine

I got the blues thinking of the future, so
I fear there will be no future for those
who do not change.
>   —Louis L'Amour

Strike when thou wilt, the hour of rest,
but let my last days be my best.
>   —Robert Browning

You learn to build your roads on today,
because tomorrow's ground is too uncertain for plans, and futures have a way of
falling down in mid-flight.
>   —Veronica Shoffstal

PART EIGHT

COURAGE

Courage Is the Foundation of All Our Virtues

Courage is the first of the human qualities because it is the quality which guarantees all the others.

—Sir Winston Churchill

The courage of life is often a less dramatic spectacle than the courage of a final moment, but it is no less a magnificent mixture of triumph and tragedy. A man does what he must—in spite of personal consequences, in spite of obstacles and dangers and pressures—and that is the basis of all morality.

—John F. Kennedy

Courage is the greatest of all the virtues. Because if you haven't courage, you may not have an opportunity to use any of the others.

—Samuel Johnson

Courage is the most important of all virtues, because without it we can't practice any other virtue with consistency.
—Maya Angelou

Courage is not simply one of the virtues, but the form of every virtue at the testing point.
—C.S. Lewis

Courage is the ladder on which all other virtues mount.
—Clare Boothe Luce

Courage is the basic virtue for everyone so long as he continues to grow, to move ahead.
—Rollo May

Nothing but courage can guide life.
—Vauvenargues

Without courage, all other virtues lose their meaning.
—Sir Winston Churchill

BOLDNESS AND BRAVERY
ARE VITAL QUALITIES

Why not go out on a limb? Isn't that
where the fruit is?

—Frank Scully

In difficult situations, when hope seems
feeble, the boldest plans are safest.

—Livy

A decent boldness ever meets with
friends.

—Homer

Attacking is the only secret. Dare and the
world always yields; or if it beats you
sometimes, dare it again, and it will suc-
cumb.

—William Makepeace Thackeray

In times of stress, be bold and valiant.

—Horace

Courage is the best slayer—courage
which attacketh, for in every attack there
is the sound of triumph.
                    —Friedrich Nietzsche

He who finds Fortune on his side should
go briskly ahead, for she is wont to favor
the bold.
                    —Baltasar Gracian

It is better by noble boldness to run the
risk of being subject to half of the evils we
anticipate than to remain in cowardly list-
lessness for fear of what might happen.
                    —Herodotus

Audacity augments courage; hesitation,
fear.
                    —Publilius Syrus

Fortune reveres the brave, and over-
whelms the cowardly.
                    —Marcus Annaeus Seneca

God helps the brave.

> —J.C.F. von Schiller

It is the bold man who every time does best, at home or abroad.

> —Homer

You don't learn to hold your own in the world by standing on guard, but by attacking, and getting well-hammered yourself.

> —George Bernard Shaw

The brave venture anything.

> —Anon.

Fortune helps the brave.

> —Virgil

Fortune befriends the bold.

> —John Dryden

Fortune and love favor the brave.

> —Ovid

Fortune favors the audacious.

—Erasmus

Audacity, more audacity, always audacity.

—Georges Jacques Danton

With audacity one can undertake anything.

—Napoleon Bonaparte

Bravery and faith bring both material and spiritual rewards.

—Preston Bradley

He who loses wealth loses much; he who loses a friend loses more; but he who loses his courage loses all.

—Miguel de Cervantes

True miracles are created by men when they use the courage and intelligence that God gave them.

—Jean Anouilh

THE COURAGE TO
FACE LIFE DIRECTLY

Success is never found. Failure is never
fatal. Courage is the only thing.
—Sir Winston Churchill

Tender-handed stroke a nettle, and it
stings you for your pains;
Grasp it like a man of mettle, and it soft
as silk remains.
—Thomas Fuller

Life is the acceptance of responsibilities,
or their evasion; it is a business of meeting obligations, or avoiding them.
—Ben Ames Williams

Facing it—always facing it—that's the
way to get through. Face it!
—Joseph Conrad

Let us be brave in the face of adversity.
—Marcus Annaeus Seneca

He shall fare well who confronts circumstances aright.

> —Plutarch

He that handles a nettle tenderly is soon-
est stung.

> —Thomas Fuller

Only one feat is possible: not to have run
away.

> —Dag Hammarskjold

There is something healthy and invigo-
rating about direct action.

> —Henry Miller

Confidence ... is directness and courage
in meeting the facts of life.

> —John Dewey

The superior man makes the difficulty to
be overcome his first interest; success
comes only later.

> —Confucius

The man who most vividly realizes a difficulty is the man most likely to overcome it.

> —Joseph Farrell

He who is afraid of every nettle should not piss in the grass.

> —Thomas Fuller

I believe half the unhappiness in life comes from people being afraid to go straight at things.

> —William J. Lock

No man will succeed unless he is ready to face and overcome difficulties, and is prepared to assume responsibilities.

> —William J.H. Boetcher

The fly that doesn't want to be swatted is most secure when it lights on the flyswatter.

> —Georg Christoph Lichtenberg

It is often wonderful how putting down on paper a clear statement of a case helps one to see, not perhaps the way out, but the way in.

—Arthur Christopher Benson

A great man is one who seizes the vital issue in a complex question, what we might call the jugular vein of the whole organism, and spends his energies upon that.

—Joseph Rickaby

Have the courage to face a difficulty lest it kick you harder than you bargain for.

—Stanislaus

Every difficulty slurred over will be a ghost to disturb your repose later on.

—Frédéric Chopin

All problems become smaller if you don't dodge them, but confront them.

—William F. Halsey

As a rule, what is out of sight disturbs
men's minds more seriously than what
they see.

—Julius Caesar

The fly ought to be used as the symbol
of impertinence and audacity, for whilst
all other animals shun man more than
anything else, and run away even before
he comes near them, the fly lights upon
his very nose.

—Arthur Schopenhauer

Life is a battle in which we fall from
wounds we receive in running away.

—William L. Sullivan

Fools, through false shame, conceal their
open wounds.

—Horace

We cannot solve life's problems except by
solving them.

—M. Scott Peck

However mean your life is, meet it and live it; do not shun it and call it hard names. It is not so bad as you are.

—Henry David Thoreau

The best way out of a problem is through it.

—Anon.

The truth will set you free, but first it will make you miserable.

—James A. Garfield

Let us not look back in anger, nor forward in fear, but around us in awareness.

—James Thurber

It takes courage to know when you ought to be afraid.

—James A. Michener

Genius is an infinite capacity for taking life by the scruff of the neck.

—Katharine Hepburn

If you suppress grief too much, it can well redouble.

—Moliere

Bad weather always looks worse through a window.

—Anon.

The frontiers are not east or west, north or south, but wherever a man fronts a fact.

—Henry David Thoreau

Should I, after tea and cakes and ices, have the strength to force the moment to its crisis?

—T.S. Eliot

You don't change the course of history by turning the faces of portraits to the wall.

—Jawaharlal Nehru

Soldiers, strike the foe in the face!

—Florus

Get in front of the ball, you won't get hurt. That's what you've got a chest for, young man.

—John McGraw

The great virtue in life is real courage that knows how to face facts and live beyond them.

—D.H. Lawrence

Knowledge of sin is the beginning of salvation.

—Marcus Annaeus Seneca

Wealth lost—something lost; Honor lost—much lost; Courage lost—all lost.

—Old German proverb

It is courage, courage, courage, that raises the blood of life to crimson splendor. Live bravely and present a brave front to adversity!

—Horace

Whatever you are trying to avoid won't
go away until you confront it.

>   —Anon.

Risk! Risk anything!... Do the hardest
thing on earth for you. Act for yourself.
Face the truth.

>   —Katherine Mansfield

The first rule is to keep an untroubled
spirit. The second is to look things in the
face and know them for what they are.

>   —Marcus Aurelius

None are so blind as those who will not
see.

>   —Anon.

Courage is a quietness, not martial music
    made
Born of facing up to life, even when
    afraid.

>   —Emily Sargent Councilman

THE COURAGE TO FACE THE TRUTH ABOUT OURSELVES

You can't expect to win unless you know why you lose.

— Benjamin Lipson

We run away all the time to avoid coming face to face with ourselves.

— Anon.

Awakening begins when a man realizes that he is going nowhere, and does not know where to go.

— Georges Gurdjieff

The man with insight enough to admit his limitations comes nearest to perfection.

— Johann von Goethe

You're only as sick as your secrets.

— Anon.

The confession of evil works is the first beginning of good works.

—Saint Augustine

Admitting errors clears the score and proves you wiser than before.

—Arthur Guiterman

An excuse is a lie guarded.

—Jonathan Swift

Honesty is the first chapter of the book of wisdom.

—Thomas Jefferson

The real gift of love is self disclosure.

—John Powell

We only really face up to ourselves when we are afraid.

—Thomas Bernhard

EMOTIONAL, SPIRITUAL, AND MENTAL COURAGE

It takes a lot of courage to show your dreams to someone else.

—Erma Bombeck

It takes more courage to reveal insecurities than to hide them, more strength to relate to people than to dominate them, more "manhood" to abide by thought-out principles rather than blind reflex. Toughness is in the soul and spirit, not in muscles and an immature mind.

—Alex Karras

I have often though morality may perhaps consist solely in the courage of making a choice.

—Leon Blum

It is easy to be brave from a safe distance.

—Aesop

This is the art of courage: to see things as they are and still believe that the victory lies not with those who avoid the bad, but those who taste, in living awareness, every drop of the good.

—Victoria Lincoln

The highest courage is to dare to appear to be what one is.

—John Lancaster Spalding

True courage is not the brutal force of vulgar heroes, but the firm resolve of virtue and reason.

—Alfred North Whitehead

Courage ... is nothing less than the power to overcome danger, misfortune, fear, injustice, while continuing to affirm inwardly that life, with all its sorrows, is good; that everything is meaningful, even if in a sense beyond our understanding; and that there is always tomorrow.

—Dorothy Thompson

Greatness, in the last analysis, is largely bravery—courage in escaping from old ideas and old standards.

—James Harvey Robinson

The highest courage is not to be found in the instinctive acts of men who risk their lives to save a friend or slay a foe; the physical fearlessness of a moment or an hour is not to be compared with immolation of months or years for the sake of wisdom or art.

—Joseph H. Odell

I have met brave women who are exploring the outer edge of human possibility, with no history to guide them, and with a courage to make themselves vulnerable that I find moving beyond words.

—Gloria Steinem

Valour is nobleness of the mind.

—Anon.

God grant me the courage not to give up what I think is right, even though I think it is hopeless.

—Admiral Chester W. Nimitz

The great virtue in life is real courage that knows how to face facts and live beyond them.

—D.H. Lawrence

Physical courage, which despises all danger, will make a man brave in one way; and moral courage, which despises all opinion, will make a man brave in another. The former would seem most necessary for the camp; the latter for the council; but to constitute a great man, both are necessary.

—Charles Caleb Colton

Courage is the power to let go of the familiar.

—Raymond Lindquist

Valor is stability, not of legs and arms,
but of courage and the soul.
—Michel de Montaigne

One of man's finest qualities is described
by the simple word "guts"—the ability to
take it. If you have the discipline to stand
fast when your body wants to run, if you
can control your temper and remain
cheerful in the face of monotony or dis-
appointment, you have "guts" in the sol-
diering sense.
—Colonel John S. Roosman

Whatever course you decide upon, there
is always someone to tell you that you
are wrong. There are always difficulties
arising which tempt you to believe that
your critics are right. To map out a
course of action and follow it to an end
requires ... courage.
—Ralph Waldo Emerson

Courage and Conviction

Courage is more than standing for a firm conviction. It includes the risk of questioning that conviction.

—Julian Weber Gordon

Courage is what it takes to stand up and speak; courage is also what it takes to sit down and listen.

—Anon.

The hallmark of courage in our age of conformity is the capacity to stand on one's convictions—not obstinately or defiantly (these are gestures of defensiveness, not courage) nor as a gesture of retaliation, but simply because these are what one believes.

—Rollo May

REACTING TO DIFFICULT SITUATIONS

The greatest test of courage on earth is to
bear defeat without losing heart.
—Robert G. Ingersoll

Courage is to take hard knocks like a
man when occasion calls.
—Plautus

This is courage ... to bear unflinchingly
what heaven sends.
—Euripides

Courage, in the final analysis, is nothing
but an affirmative answer to the shocks
of existence.
—Dr. Kurt Goldstein

Courage is a perfect sensibility of the
measure of danger, and a mental willingness to endure it.
—General William T. Sherman

One man with courage makes a majority.
—Andrew Jackson

To have courage for whatever comes in
life—everything lies in that.
—Saint Teresa of Avila

To accept whatever comes, regardless of
the consequences, is to be unafraid.
—John Cage

The test of courage comes when we are
in the minority.
—Ralph W. Sockman

Courage and perseverance have a magical
talisman, before which difficulties disap-
pear, and obstacles vanish into air.
—John Quincy Adams

We need the courage to start and continue what we should do, and courage to
stop what we shouldn't do.
—Richard L. Evans

COURAGE AND HAPPINESS

Many women miss their greatest chance
of happiness through a want of courage
in a decisive moment.
—Winifred Gordon

We must have the courage to be happy.
—Henri Frederic Amiel

There is a courage of happiness as well as
a courage of sorrow.
—Maurice Maeterlinck

Happy the man who ventures boldly to
defend what he holds dear.
—Ovid

We must have courage to bet on our
ideas, on the calculated risk, and to act.
Everyday living requires courage if life is
to be effective and bring happiness.
—Maxwell Maltz

All happiness depends on courage and work.

—Honore de Balzac

There is nothing in the world so much admired as a man who knows how to bear unhappiness with courage.

—Marcus Annaeus Seneca

Faint heart never won fair lady.

—Miguel de Cervantes

The last thing a woman will consent to discover in a man whom she loves, or on whom she simply depends, is want of courage.

—Joseph Conrad

None but the brave deserve the fair.

—John Dryden

Fortune and love favor the brave.

—Ovid

Courage and Conflict

The weapon of the brave is in his heart.
—Anon.

The guts carry the feet, not the feet the guts.
—Miguel de Cervantes

War is fear cloaked in courage.
—General William Westmoreland

A bold heart is half the battle.
—Anon.

Courage in danger is half the battle.
—Plautus

A man of courage never wants weapons.
—Anon.

A brave arm makes a short sword long.
—Anon.

Courage which goes against military expediency is stupidity, or, if it is insisted upon by a commander, irresponsibility.

—General Erwin Rommel

To say yes, you have to sweat and roll up your sleeves and plunge both hands into life up to the elbows. It is easy to say no, even if saying no means death.

—Jean Anouilh

There is, in addition to a courage with which men die, a courage by which men must live.

—John F. Kennedy

Have the courage to live. Anyone can die.

—Robert Cody

Only those are fit to live who are not afraid to die.

—General Douglas MacArthur

Where life is more terrible than death, it
is the truest valor to dare to live.

—Sir Thomas Browne

The courage we desire and prize is not
the courage to die decently, but to live
manfully.

—Thomas Carlyle

Often the test of courage is not to die,
but to live.

—Conte Vittorio Alfieri

He who has the courage to laugh is
almost as much the master of the world
as he who is ready to die.

—Giacomo Leopardi

Sometimes even to live is an act of
courage.

—Marcus Annaeus Seneca

Life shrinks or expands in proportion to
one's courage.

—Anaïs Nin

We Can't Succeed
without Courage

Because a fellow has failed once or twice
or a dozen times, you don't want to set
him down as a failure till he's dead or
loses his courage—and that's the same
thing.

—George Horace Lorimer

What is more mortifying than to feel
that you have missed the plum for want
of courage to shake the tree?

—Logan Pearsall Smith

It takes vision and courage to create—it
takes faith and courage to prove.

—Owen D. Young

Whatever you do, you need courage....
To map out a course of action and follow
it to an end requires some of the same
courage which a soldier needs.

—Ralph Waldo Emerson

Who dares nothing, need hope for nothing.

> —J.C.F. von Schiller

Have the courage of your desire.

> —George R. Gissing

To see what is right, and not do it, is want of courage.

> —Confucius

No great thing comes to any man unless he has courage.

> —Cardinal James Gibbons

Great things are done more through courage than through wisdom.

> —German proverb

Courage permits the caliber of performance to continue at its peak, until the finish line is crossed.

> —Stuart Walker

Failure is only postponed success as long as courage "coaches" ambition. The habit of persistence is the habit of victory.

—Herbert Kaufman

There are a lot of fellas with all the ability it takes to play in the major leagues, but ... they always get stuck in the minor leagues because they haven't got the guts to make the climb.

—Cookie Lavagetto

You will never do anything in this world without courage.

—James Lane Allen

The bravest are the tenderest. The loving are the daring.

—Henry Wadsworth Longfellow

Where there is a brave man, in the thickest of the fight, there is the post of honor.

—Henry David Thoreau

It takes as much courage to have tried and failed as it does to have tried and succeeded.

—Anne Morrow Lindbergh

Whenever you see a successful business, someone once made a courageous decision.

—Peter Drucker

Courage to start and willingness to keep everlasting at it are the requisites for success.

—Alonzo Newton Benn

One of the biggest factors in success is the courage to undertake something.

—James A. Worsham

What would life be if we had no courage to attempt anything?

—Vincent van Gogh

WITHOUT COURAGE, ABILITY AND TALENT WON'T BE ENOUGH

Everyone has a talent. What is rare is the courage to follow that talent to the dark place where it leads.

—Erica Jong

The world is not perishing for the want of clever or talented or well-meaning men. It is perishing for the want of men of courage and resolution.

—Robert J. McCracken

Knowledge without courage is sterile.

—Baltasar Gracian

Courage is the thing. All goes if courage goes.

—Sir James M. Barrie

WE MUST HAVE
THE COURAGE TO BEGIN

Nothing ventured, nothing gained.
—Anon.

It's weak and despicable to go on wanting
things and not trying to get them.
—Joanna Field

How many feasible projects have miscar-
ried through despondency, and been
strangled in their birth by a cowardly
imagination?
—Jeremy Collier

One of the biggest factors in success is
the courage to undertake something.
—James A. Worsham

When it comes to betting on yourself ...
you're a chicken-livered coward if you
hesitate.
—B.C. Forbes

Be courageous!... I have seen many depressions in business. Always America has come out stronger and more prosperous. Be as brave as your fathers before you. Have faith! Go forward.

—Thomas A. Edison

Dare to begin! He who postpones living rightly is like the rustic who waits for the river to run out before he crosses.

—Horace

The brave venture anything.

—Anon.

You can surmount the obstacles in your path if you are determined, courageous and hardworking.... Do not fear to pioneer, to venture down new paths of endeavor.

—Ralph J. Bunche

Life is to be entered upon with courage.
—Alexis de Tocqueville

The difference between getting somewhere and nowhere is the courage to
make an early start.

—Charles M. Schwab

We ought to face our destiny with
courage.

—Friedrich Nietzsche

The great man is the man who does a
thing for the first time.

—Alexander Smith

Imposing limitations on yourself is cowardly because it protects you from having
to try, and perhaps failing.

—Vladimir Zworykin

What you can do, or dream you can do,
begin it; boldness has genius, power and
magic in it.

—Johann von Goethe

COURAGE AND FEAR

When you're my size in the pros, fear is a
sign that you're not stupid.

—Jerry Levias

Keep your fears to yourself, but share
your courage with others.

—Robert Louis Stevenson

Courage leads starward, fear toward
death.

—Marcus Annaeus Seneca

Go forth to meet the shadowy Future
without fear and with a manly heart.

—Henry Wadsworth Longfellow

Fate loves the fearless.

—James Russell Lowell

There is no such thing as bravery, only
degrees of fear.

—John Wainwright

Courage is a peculiar kind of fear.
—Charles Kennedy

You look at a guy who's being brave. He's afraid, or he wouldn't be brave. If he isn't afraid, he's stupid.
—Joe Torre

Courage is knowing what not to fear.
—Plato

To fight a bull when you are not scared is nothing. And to not fight a bull when you are scared is nothing. But to fight a bull when you are scared is something.
—Anon.

Courage is fear that has said its prayers.
—Dorothy Bernard

Courage is doing what you're afraid to do. There can be no courage unless you're scared.
—Eddie Rickenbacker

Being "brave" means doing or facing something frightening.... Being "fearless" means being without fear.

—Penelope Leach

Courage is fear holding on a minute longer.

—General George S. Patton

Courage is being scared to death ... and saddling up anyway.

—John Wayne

Courage is a scorner of things which inspire fear.

—Marcus Annaeus Seneca

We must constantly build dykes of courage to hold back the flood of fear.

—Martin Luther King, Jr.

Courage is the ability to solve problems realistically in the presence of fear.

—Stuart Walker

DREAMS FUEL COURAGE

Courage is sustained by calling up anew
the vision of the goal.

> —A.G. Sertillanges

Optimism is the foundation of courage.

> —Nicholas Murray Butler

No one has yet computed how many
imaginary triumphs are silently celebrated by people each year to keep up
their courage.

> —Henry S. Haskins

Courage is like love, it must have hope
for nourishment.

> —Napoleon Bonaparte

Courage does not always march to airs
blown by a bugle, it is not always
wrought out of the fabric ostentation
wears.

> —Frances Rodman

OTHER DEFINITIONS OF COURAGE

Courage is as often the outcome of
despair as of hope; in the one case we
have nothing to lose, in the other everything to gain.

—Diane De Pottiers

Courage does not consist in calculation,
but in fighting against chances.

—John Henry Cardinal Newman

Courage is its own reward.

—Plautus

Courage is the price that life exacts for
granting peace.

—Amelia Earhart

Courage is a kind of salvation.

—Plato

Courage is grace under pressure.

—Ernest Hemingway

Courage that grows from constitution often forsakes a man ... courage which arises from a sense of duty acts in a uniform manner.

—Joseph Addison

Courage is the lovely virtue—the rib of Himself that God sent down to His children.

—Sir James M. Barrie

Courage is the integrating strength that causes one to overcome tragedy.

—Eugene E. Brussell

Courage is almost a contradiction in terms. It means a strong desire to live taking the form of readiness to die.

—G.K. Chesterton

Courage is the virtue which champions the cause of right.

—Cicero

Courage is required not only in a person's occasional crucial decision for his own freedom, but in the little hour-to-hour decisions which place the bricks in the structure of his building of himself into a person who acts with freedom and responsibility.

—Rollo May

We learn courageous action by going forward whenever fear urges us back.

—David Seabury

If we survive danger, it steels our courage more than anything else.

—Reinhold Niebuhr

It takes courage to live—courage and strength and hope and humor. And courage and strength and hope and humor have to be bought and paid for with pain and work and prayers and tears.

—Jerome P. Fleishman

He who knows how to suffer everything
can dare everything.

—Vauvenargues

The paradox of courage is that a man
must be a little careless of his life in order
to keep it.

—G.K. Chesterton

How, then, find the courage for action?
By slipping a little into unconsciousness,
spontaneity, instinct which holds one to
the earth and dictates the relatively good
and useful.... By accepting the human
condition more simply, and candidly, by
dreading troubles less, calculating less,
hoping more.

—Henri Frederic Amiel

Courage is generosity of the highest
order, for the brave are prodigal of the
most precious things.

—Charles Caleb Colton